Homosexuality

The Bible on Trial

David Robert-John

authorHOUSE®

AuthorHouse™
1663 Liberty Drive
Bloomington, IN 47403
www.authorhouse.com
Phone: 1-800-839-8640

Except where otherwise indicated All Scripture quotations in this publication are from THE HOLY BIBLE, NEW INTERNATIONAL VERSION®, NIV® Copyright © 1973, 1978, 1984, 2011 by Biblica, Inc.™ Used by permission. All rights reserved worldwide.

Scripture quotations denoted with (RSV) are from the Revised Standard Version of the Bible, copyright 1952 [2nd edition, 1971] by the Division of Christian Education of the National Council of the Churches of Christ in the United States of America. Used by permission. All rights reserved."

The author wishes to acknowledge the use of Mohammad Marmaduke Pickthall's translation of the Qu'rân published by Albirr Foundation UK (he understands that the material has no copyright attached to it) Also the Patterson and Meyer translation of the Gospel of Thomas (the author was unable to establish if this material has copyright).

Published by AuthorHouse   03/14/2012

ISBN: 978-1-4678-8600-0 (sc)
ISBN: 978-1-4678-8601-7 (e)

Dedication

To my wife and my three surviving children.
I love you all

Also

To all those who have preceded me in the search for religious truth and have written books that have influenced my own thoughts. Some of their ideas may well be contained in this, my own offering to that quest.

Contents

Acknowledgements

I am indebted, once again, to the following people for their continued interest, advice, help and support:

David Callaghan
David Stokes
Helen Collins
Roderick Thomson

Preface

My first book dealt with the conflict between my Bible-believing Christian faith and the homosexuality of one of my sons. It explained why I eventually came to believe that the Bible's view of homosexuality was wrong. This had enormous implications for me as it meant that the Bible could not be the inerrant Word of God that, for over forty years of my life, I had assumed it to be. If that was the case, just how far could any of it be trusted? And what implications would this have for Christian belief? This book attempts to investigate these questions and to provide an answer.

The views put forward are those that I have formed as a result of my own studies of the Bible over many years, but a number them are the result of the intensive study that I made following my son's coming out. However, I have read many books in my lifetime and I have obviously taken on board some of the ideas that I came across. I cannot, therefore, claim that all my views are original. Indeed, it would be a surprise if most, or even all, of the ideas expressed here have not been aired before, probably many times, in serious academic circles.

Unfortunately, specialists have the habit of talking among themselves and ignoring the rest of us. This book has been written for ordinary, non-specialist readers who nevertheless have an interest in religion and truth. Its central claim is that the confidence that many Christians place in the authority of the Bible is sadly misplaced and that, in any case, the Bible narratives offer only the flimsiest support for traditional Christian belief. This has enormous consequences for the Church's views regarding homosexuality, views that, in my opinion, should be challenged in the strongest possible manner.

Except where otherwise indicated, quotations are taken from the New International Version of the Bible because this seemed to be generally accepted in the charismatic church that I attended. However, I was accustomed to use the Revised Standard Version in my younger days and I still find a number of its passages to be more poetic than many of the modern versions. Where use of the RSV version is indicated, therefore, it simply shows my preference for the way it renders the passage concerned. In no instance does any argument put forward depend on a particular translation

I have used the more modern convention of BCE and CE rather than BC and AD for dates. There is no particular reason for this and I do not subscribe to political correctness, but it does seem that it is becoming more common to use this notation.

David Robert-John (Jan 2012)

1 THE BIBLE: A TRUSTWORTHY BOOK?

We live in a world where countless millions of people base their beliefs and their lives around the teachings contained in a particular book, a book that they consider to be divinely inspired. The Bible and the Qu'rân are the two principal books in this category and they exert enormous influence over the lives of Christians (particularly those of evangelical or fundamentalist persuasion) and Muslims respectively.

Given the influence that these books have, we are entitled to ask if it is it rational, or even reasonable, to base our beliefs on the texts contained in either of them. What follows is largely concerned with the Bible because Christian beliefs are based on what it teaches and these beliefs were a great part of my life for so long. It is the realm with which I am most familiar and in which I have the greatest interest, although some reference is also made to the Qu'rân.

The New Testament is the part of the Bible that provides us with the basis for Christian belief. In examining the credibility of the Bible, I have looked at the credibility of one particular part of the New Testament, the four Gospels and the Acts of the Apostles, to find out just how much unequivocal support they offer for the beliefs held by millions of Christians.

It is rather surprising in the circumstances to find that most believers almost certainly do not have the slightest idea on what grounds they believe the Bible to be "the truth" except for the fact that Jesus clearly held the Old Testament writings with which he was familiar to be the Word of God. The New Testament, of course, did not exist when Jesus lived. The views of most believers are, in fact, based on what other people think about the Bible. Most of us are guilty of assuming that more knowledgeable people than ourselves have vouched for its veracity and therefore we are entitled place our own faith in it with confidence. Surely, Christian belief would not have survived for two thousand years unless there was overwhelming evidence for its message?

The reality, however, is that a huge edifice has been built up over the centuries, one that in many ways resembles an inverted pyramid. It consists of layer upon layer of people whose beliefs are based on the beliefs of people in a layer below them. If we travel back far enough in time, we end up with a tiny base which represents the earliest believers, the very small number of people who must have had a fairly intimate knowledge of Jesus during the time of his ministry. Faith began with this small group, spread, and has been transmitted from generation to generation ever since. Very few people are aware of the enormous problems that the New Testament narratives present, and it must be said that not many people seem to care.

The beliefs of the earliest Christians could not have been based on any kind of intellectual conviction. Certainly, once Christianity had spread beyond the immediate confines of Judaism, hardly any of the new believers would have known Jesus or have had much knowledge of the Jewish Old Testament Scriptures. Their faith would have rested on the credibility of people such as St. Paul and the emotional appeal of his message.

In one sense, little has changed since those days. People's faith, at least initially, usually rests on the credibility of those who shared the Gospel with them. They "buy into" the beliefs that these people have and hardly any, from there on, make a real effort to examine the ground on which these beliefs have been constructed. This is, in many ways, understandable. The Gospel message may be relatively simple: you are offered forgiveness, a fresh start and a life-transforming relationship with the God who created the universe, together with eternal salvation, in exchange for placing your trust in his son, Jesus. The credibility of all this, however, is by no means easy to assess. Most people do not have the time to engage in a rigorous examination of the validity of their beliefs and so they are encouraged, instead, to rely on their "experience" of God, and the fact that millions of others have taken the same step and, they are assured, have not been disappointed. Human beings, unfortunately, are gullible and susceptible to huge amounts of self-delusion. We can convince ourselves of almost anything, particularly if we imagine that our beliefs will bring some tangible benefit to our lives.

Today, we have one significant advantage over the earliest believers. We have ready access to the documents upon which Christian beliefs are supposed to be based. These documents reflect belief about Jesus at the time that they were written down. A study of them, particularly of the four Gospels and of the Acts of the Apostles, provides a basis on which we can make some kind of objective assessment of the credibility of the beliefs that we may have committed ourselves to.

I must acknowledge that I had to retire before I found the time necessary for such a project. I was also provided with a massive incentive to undertake this task. The knowledge that one of my children was gay put my beliefs of more than forty years on trial. I needed answers, and I needed them desperately. This was no longer merely an academic or a theological issue for me. The people amongst whom I had spent most of my life regarded my son, or at least his lifestyle, as an abomination. Were they right to do so? Was the Bible, the book to which they ascribe such authority, worthy of this esteem? Was it really the Word of God?

I was determined, if at all possible, to discover some credible answers to these questions. I could not afford the luxury of waiting until the afterlife; I needed answers now, in my lifetime, when they would have some relevance. I had, for most of my life, harboured some doubts about the claims made for the Bible and it was now a matter of urgency that I made an effort to resolve these concerns. Further, I had always been surrounded by people who seemed to have no interest in such matters and who could not understand my own preoccupation with them. Why could I not just accept the faith and believe what I had been told? The basic assumption always seemed to be that any questioning of established beliefs was an affront to God and would inevitably bring its own judgement.

I was, of course, well aware that many others, people with far greater intellectual capacity and far more spiritual depth than I possessed, had probably engaged in a similar task in an attempt to discover deeper meaning and a more complete version of the truth. To the best of my knowledge, they had all died without arriving at this Holy Grail. Or, if they had managed to reach a satisfactory conclusion to their quest, I am not aware of any clues that they may have left behind to help those of us trying to follow in their footsteps. Why would I imagine that I could succeed where so many others seemed to have failed?

As I began my quest, I was by no means certain that there would be an answer to that question, and I now know that if it had not been for one issue, I would have joined all the others and would have gone to my grave with my misgivings unresolved. The issue in question was that of homosexuality and it proved to be the key to unlocking the secret that I had been searching for. This is because, without this intrusion into my life, I would never have entertained the possibility that the Bible was not the Word of God and I would have gone on searching for answers that did not exist in the form I had imagined. This is why so many others before me had searched in vain. Homosexuality has only been a serious, contentious issue in the last thirty years or so. Without this key, they would have carried out the search with a set of preconceived conditions attached, the very opposite of what we would now consider to be scientific or valid research. In other words, the possibility that the Bible was not the Word of God was not within the scope of their investigations.

One question above all others, regarding the New Testament story, had been a constant source of bewilderment, uncertainty and angst for me. It concerned an incident recorded by Luke in Acts 3:1-8. Peter and John, on their way to the temple to pray, are confronted by a crippled beggar wanting money. Peter's response was to say to the beggar, "*Silver or gold I do not have, but what I have I give you. In the Name of Jesus Christ of Nazareth, walk.*" There are three little words in that sentence which clearly separated my experience of Christianity, and everybody else's, from that of the apostle Peter: the words "*what I have.*" Peter did not offer to pray for the man's healing. He appeared to know that he possessed the power to heal him, a power no doubt bestowed upon him when he was "baptised in the Holy Spirit" on the day of Pentecost. Perhaps this was also fulfilling a promise of Jesus in John 14:12: "*I tell you the truth, anyone who has faith in me will do what I have been doing. He will do even greater things than these, because I am going to the Father.*"

It is clear that neither the "Baptism with the Holy Spirit" nor the ability to perform the kind of "signs" that Jesus performed, were intended to be restricted to the immediate disciples of Jesus. The Acts of the Apostles subsequently tells us of a man named Stephen who "*did great wonders and miraculous signs among the people*" (Acts 6:8). We are not told that Stephen was ever acquainted with the living Jesus. Why did these people in the early Church have access to powers that appear to have been promised to all believers when nobody seems to have access to such powers today? Was there any answer to this question? And if not, what were the implications?

Why, it might be asked, does any of this matter if Christianity has served us well for two thousand years and millions of people still derive great comfort from its beliefs? There are two answers to this question. The first is to point out that Christianity is alright provided that you are not homosexual. There happens to be a group of people who, from no choice of their own, are homosexual and who, therefore, are excluded from any of the benefits of this faith. It is a simple question of justice. And justice demands that the confident assertions made by many Christians (and also by some vote-seeking politicians) regarding the issue of homosexuality are subjected to serious scrutiny. Second, there is the issue of truth. Should we encourage false beliefs on the grounds that some people may find them to be beneficial?

One trait that is characteristic of part of the human race at least is a desire for knowledge and truth. It may not be a universal trait and I know many people who have little interest in such matters providing that they are happy with their lives. But progress would not be possible unless a sufficient number of human beings did have a desire for these things. I must belong to this latter group because, for almost as long as I can remember, I have been obsessed with the questions "How?" and "Why?"

A desire for knowledge and truth cannot be circumscribed by preconceived ideas, by what I would like the truth to be. Truth is something that is independent of my beliefs or anyone else's. To discover the truth is to discover reality and I must accept whatever that reality turns out to be. I am not a traitor because I have come to change my mind about my religious beliefs. I am simply someone who came to realise that certain realities were in conflict with my most deeply held beliefs and that the two could not be reconciled. Honesty and integrity, in the end, forced me to recognise that fact.

What I write, therefore, is for those who are also interested in the truth regarding one of the most important and all-pervasive aspects of human life: our religious beliefs. I would also hope that there would be some believers who are sufficiently sure of their beliefs to risk exposing them to some very awkward questions, even if they do not, in the end, agree with my conclusions.

I am now convinced that homophobia exists in the Church because of ignorance and bigotry, both of which stem from an uncritical belief in the infallibility of the Bible. Ultimately, truth can withstand any attempt to discredit it. Both the Bible and Christianity, if they represent the truth, will be able to refute arguments advanced against their credibility. The foundation upon which this credibility rests, however, should be rock solid; it should not be merely a matter of unquestioning, blind belief.

Once I had retired I set about reading and re-reading the Gospels and the Acts of the Apostles in order to see if I could find any clues as to why there was a gap between my beliefs and my experience. This time, however, I was no longer reading through faith-tinted spectacles and at some stage during this process, something dawned on me regarding Luke's accounts of the events following the Resurrection and the formation of the early Church as recorded in the first few chapters of Acts. It was to be a crucial insight that eventually would undermine all of my orthodox Christian beliefs. Just as Herodotus, the Greek historian and the man regarded as the father of history is said to have done, I realised that Luke might, conceivably, have invented material when he did not know the facts or when he could conveniently simplify the narrative to provide a coherent explanation for the existence of the Church that he had come to know.

Luke's accounts of the Virgin Birth, the Resurrection, the Ascension and the events on the day of Pentecost all appeared to have considerable question marks hanging over them. When we add this to the fact that two of the miracles recorded in John's Gospel give rise to serious doubt and the accounts of the Transfiguration also raise a significant problem, we are left facing the fact that none of the events that would mark Jesus as being the unique Son of God find unequivocal support in the New Testament.

I shall deal with each of these difficulties in some detail in the following chapters, beginning with the Virgin Birth because I am reminded of something that I was taught at university: the importance of beginnings. If the initial equations relating to a problem are formulated incorrectly, then nothing that follows has any relevance. A mistake at the beginning will lead to a false answer, no matter how good the mathematics from there on. If the doctrine of the Virgin Birth rests on very shaky foundations, it is bound to give rise to serious questions about everything else that follows, particularly any assumption about the divine nature of Jesus.

2   THE VIRGIN BIRTH

When we consider doctrines that are central to the Christian faith, we are entitled to expect that support for belief in these doctrines would be total and of the "cast-iron" variety. This means that we are dealing with issues of such importance that every account of the life of Jesus would be expected to include some mention of them. The failure to make any reference to a particular doctrine, in any Gospel, should be enough at least to raise our suspicions. The Virgin Birth is a prime example. If it was true, it would be a unique event of such magnitude that every convert to the faith would have come to know about it. No writer of any of the Gospels could have imagined that it was of insufficient importance to warrant inclusion in an account of Jesus's life.

This is not, however, the case. What we find is that only two of the four Gospel writers make any specific mention of it and their accounts are not only different but so full of fantasy as to place them in the "most unlikely" category. Mark's Gospel not only makes no mention of it but includes a passage that makes the whole idea of a Virgin Birth seem highly improbable. The particular verse in question is Mark 3:21 where we are told that: "*When his family heard about this, they went to take charge of him, for they said, 'He is out of his mind.'*" His family included his mother, as verse 31 makes clear. Mark's Gospel is commonly believed to be the first to have been written and the fact that there is no reference to a Virgin Birth strongly suggests that it was certainly written before such a belief had surfaced.

If there is any truth in the Virgin Birth stories, Mary could never have entertained any doubts about her son. A visitation from an angel and the event of a birth without sex are not things that she is likely to have forgotten with time. Yet here she is, concerned that he has gone mad. She would have had every reason for this concern in the natural course of events. Jesus had wasted no time in falling foul of possibly the most powerful religious group of his day, the Pharisees, by his failure to observe the Sabbath day in the accepted manner. On account of this they were already seeking ways to kill him (Mark 3:6). He was almost certainly risking expulsion from the synagogue, and this would have entailed social ostracism, not just for him, but possibly for his entire family—an absolute disaster for a Jewish family living in a small, intensely religious community. It is little wonder, then, that his family were full of anxiety.

The other Gospel that makes no mention of the Virgin Birth is that of John, generally considered to be the last of the canonical Gospels to be written. John's account, however, does refer to a curious incident that occurred at the time of the crucifixion. Jesus commits the care of his mother to the "*disciple whom he loved*" (John 19:26-27) and this has always been understood as being St. John himself. This is strange because Mary had other children, including sons, according to protestant translations of the Bible. Why was it necessary for Jesus to entrust the care of his mother to someone outside the family? And if this incident did occur, then would not John, above all others, have become privy to the supposed events surrounding the birth of Jesus? Are we to assume that Mary lived in the care of John but never confided to him the details of the miraculous birth?

What is even more disconcerting is that John's Gospel was written with a very specific objective in mind: "*But these are written that you may believe that Jesus is the Christ, the Son of God*" he says (John 20:31). Why would John omit one of the most compelling pieces of evidence that would underline Jesus's claim to uniqueness if he had been aware of it? It is not the only compelling piece of evidence that he surprisingly omits to mention as we shall see later, raising the question of whether this Gospel might not have been written by the disciple, as is claimed in the penultimate verse (21:24). If it was, we must conclude that the Virgin Birth stories were not part of the original beliefs about Jesus. If it wasn't, then there are further problems concerning the extent of eye-witness evidence.

Matthew and Luke, where we do find accounts of the Virgin Birth, also refer to the particular incident in the life of Jesus that Mark records (Matthew 12:46-50; Luke 8:19-21). Neither of them, significantly, makes any mention of the reason for the family's visit. Did they realise that if they had done so, if they had included the reason that Mark gives, it would have completely undermined their accounts of the Incarnation?

Luke's version of the Incarnation has a magical quality to it and it is surely one of the most beautiful stories ever written. To regard it as fact, however, raises problems. The story begins when God sends the angel Gabriel, first to visit Zechariah in the temple at Jerusalem, prior to the birth of John the Baptist, and then to Nazareth to visit a virgin girl named Mary. Since there were no other witnesses to either of these events (although Zechariah was struck dumb as a result of his lack of faith, a fact that would have been evidence of some unusual occurrence), we are obliged to rely on the reported testimony of each recipient of the angelic visits. Perhaps we feel able to trust Mary's word alone on account of our perceptions of her. Surely, a person as exalted as Mary has become would not invent such a story? The implications of believing that she might have done so are best left alone. However, in saying this, we are making an assumption for which we have little evidence. We cannot guarantee that Mary was the source of either of the Virgin Birth stories.

Even if there had been a Virgin Birth, it would not have been in the interests of Mary or Joseph to broadcast an event that would have made them the subject of ridicule and suspicion. There would not have been any incentive to publicise it before the Resurrection, by which time Joseph appears to have been dead, leaving Mary as the sole witness. Had the Resurrection occurred, however, then all reason for discretion would have vanished. It would have been in the interests of both Mary and her son if she was now to unveil the truth. Anything that she claimed about Jesus would have been believed without question. It would have led to an exalted status for Mary as well as providing conclusive evidence that Jesus was indeed the Son of God. And it would most certainly have meant that the story would have become well-known by every convert to the movement.

None of this, however, appears to have occurred. Far from being venerated in her own lifetime, Mary completely disappears from the scene after a brief mention in Acts 1:14, where she is among the disciples in Jerusalem awaiting the promise of the Holy Spirit. The veneration of Mary is not evident in any Bible narrative but owes its existence to the incredible thirst in the human soul for all things supernatural, as well as the belief in the Roman Catholic Church that things that are not can be transformed into things that are by the issue of a papal bull.

Thus, if the Virgin Birth and the Resurrection had both occurred, then the Virgin Birth would have become a universally known fact and Mary, as the mother of this extraordinary person who had conquered death, would surely have been revered within the nascent Jesus movement. Since the last two things did not happen, the most obvious conclusion is that the Virgin Birth and the Resurrection could not both have occurred and that, in all probability, neither of them occurred.

We are also faced with the uncomfortable problem that when Muhammad makes exactly the same claim, that the angel Gabriel appeared to him on Mt. Hirâ (near Mecca) and spoke to him, essentially entrusting him with message of the Qur'ân, Christians react with incredulity, if not something far worse. Is this not inconsistent?

Luke includes another angelic visit in his narrative, this time by an unnamed angel to the shepherds who were in the fields keeping a night-time watch over their flocks, and this is immediately followed by the appearance of "*a great company of the heavenly host*" praising God (Luke 2:8-14). The idea of an angel and the hosts of heaven choosing to announce the birth of a Saviour to simple shepherds abiding in their fields at night certainly helps to conjure up feelings of awe and wonder, as indeed does the idea of God choosing a simple peasant girl to be the mother of his son. When I think of the Christmas story, these are the abiding images that I have. But is this reality?

Do I seriously believe in the existence of angelic visitations? Are they not in the same category as the fairies that, in 1917, made an "appearance" to two girls at the bottom of a garden in Cottingley, a village in Yorkshire? The appearance of these fairies was supported by five photographs. There were many who fully believed this story, including Sir Arthur Conan Doyle, the creator of Sherlock Holmes, who referred to them in an article he wrote in 1920. In the early 1980s, Elsie Wright and Frances Griffith, the two girls involved, admitted to having faked the photographs.

Their story was believed by the same sort of people who believe in ghosts, aliens, horoscopes, tarot cards and all sorts of other superstitious nonsense. In Luke's day, and in the days of Muhammad, the world would have been full of such people, and in the case of angels or evil spirits, nobody would have thought twice to question their reality. Today, we have to ask ourselves serious questions. And serious answers will cast considerable doubt over the authenticity of Luke's account, no matter how much a part of our cultural heritage it has become.

In Luke's Gospel, angels make other appearances at events of major importance, one such occasion being to announce the Resurrection where "*two men whose clothes gleamed like lightning*" suddenly stood beside the women who had gone to the tomb (Luke 24:4). Later in the same chapter this encounter is referred to as a "vision of angels" (v 23). Already, actual encounters and visions appear to be blurred in the author's mind. At the Ascension of Jesus, told in Acts chapter 1 (also apparently written by Luke), "*two men dressed in white* [angels?] *stood beside them* [the disciples]" immediately following Jesus's disappearance from view. In chapter 12, an angel appears to Peter while he is in prison and miraculously releases him.

Luke clearly inhabited a world where angelic appearances were common, but this, while once it might have added to the credibility of a story, can now hardly be regarded as doing so. Even if Luke invented all of this material, he clearly does not seem to regard it as outside the realm of possibility. This, unfortunately, leaves us with the problem of deciding where fact ends and fantasy begins. Equally unfortunately, it seems as if there might have been a great deal of invention as well as fantasy involved in Luke's narratives. We shall see just how much a little later on.

Matthew's gospel has a totally different account of the Incarnation. Matthew was almost certainly a Jew whereas Luke appears to have been a Gentile, or at best a convert to Judaism. It is unlikely that he could conceive of God communicating directly with a woman. His world was a world created for, and dominated by, men. Eve had not been created for the benefit of God or even for her own benefit, but for the benefit of Adam. She was almost some form of afterthought. Women were deemed unfit to enter the inner temple courts in Jerusalem and no doubt equally unfit to receive messages from heaven.

Whatever the truth, Matthew's story has the angel appear to Joseph, not to Mary, and in a dream, not in reality. The importance that would have been attached to dreams in those days is mentioned later in connection with the Resurrection. He makes no mention of lowly shepherds but has men of great importance, coming from the east (Persia/modern day Iran?), bearing expensive gifts, gifts fit for an infant king. We must not forget that the Jews had once been part of the great Persian Empire that ruled from 537 BCE until the conquests of Alexander the Great in 332 BCE, a period of just over two hundred years. No doubt they had absorbed a considerable amount of Persian culture in that time, including matters of astrology. Hence he includes the story of a guiding star, the star of Bethlehem.

Stars, in Matthew's world, were tiny points of light that twinkled in the night sky. His imagination, no doubt, could easily conceive of such an object coming down to the Earth and resting over some particular spot to signify the birth of an infant king. We now know that all stars are huge. Jupiter, the largest planet in our solar system, is over three hundred times more massive than the Earth. Nevertheless, its mass would need to be more than fifty times greater than this before it could become a star. It would then be so hot that if it came anywhere near the Earth, we would not survive. Matthew was blissfully unaware of any such a drawback to his story.

The story of the star, linked to the visit of the wise men from the East, is, in turn, linked to the story of the slaughter of the infant children of Bethlehem by King Herod the Great. This has given Herod a particularly bad name. Herod, however, was simply a typical ruler of his time, a gifted but ruthless tyrant. He was probably little different from many modern day rulers. He was certainly an extraordinary builder and probably did a great deal to put his rather backward state on the map. His many magnificent projects included a huge enlargement of the temple in Jerusalem, making it one of the greatest temples in the ancient world. Not even that, however, could endear him to Matthew. Herod was simply not a bona fide Jew.

Matthew is clearly concerned to link Jesus with the royal line of David, the greatest of all Jewish kings, for his theology is rooted in the book of the prophet Isaiah, where God promises to establish the throne of his servant David for ever (Isaiah 9:7). He also draws on a prophecy found in Isaiah 7:14: "*Behold, a **virgin** shall conceive and bear a son, and shall call his name Immanuel*" [emphasis added]. To Matthew, the birth of Jesus is the fulfilment of this prophecy. There are, however, serious misgivings among many scholars regarding the reliability of the translation of the word for virgin.

The earliest extant manuscript of Isaiah that we possess is the one that was found amongst the Dead Sea Scrolls at Qumran in 1947. The version is in ancient Hebrew and many scholars insist that the Hebrew implies nothing more than "young woman". The earliest Greek manuscripts available, traditionally translated by seventy Jewish scholars in the Egyptian city of Alexandria, but presumably done over many years, probably from around 300 BCE to 150 BCE, do use the specific Greek word for virgin. Matthew, who wrote in Greek, was almost certainly quoting the Greek version that would have been more familiar to both him and his intended audience.

Prior to 1947, all Bible translations had to rely on the early Greek manuscripts, and consequently, all translations were rendered as "virgin" and not "young woman". In 1952, the Revised Standard Version of the entire Bible was first published. This version was the first to have access to the translation of Isaiah from Dead Sea Scrolls and, as far as I am aware, was the first English version to use the phrase "young woman" instead of "virgin". The complete Good News Bible, first published in 1976, is a much more modern version, and also uses the phrase "young woman." Both versions are condemned in most of the evangelical world and dismissed as the work of liberal theologians. The word "liberal" is always used in a very derogatory manner by evangelicals. It usually means an unbeliever or, at best, a very inadequate believer.

This is very revealing. It shows that even in the world of Christianity, truth can be subordinated to vested interests or can be obscured by pre-existing beliefs. In other words, we are not able to view the matter in an objective light. Our beliefs affect our ability to view issues impartially. Translations must be made to fit in with what is already believed. There is no room for any evidence which might compromise accepted dogma. However, it hardly inspires confidence when translations of crucial passages cannot be agreed upon and hence cannot be guaranteed.

This issue of belief plagues every attempt to arrive at the truth. Once people have been conditioned to see things from a certain point of view, it is almost impossible to reverse that process. New information cannot be taken on board. Max Planck's observation on scientific theories, that "*a new scientific truth does not triumph by convincing its opponents and making them see the light, but rather because its opponents eventually die, and a new generation grows up that is familiar with it*" is equally true in the world of religion. Believers who have become accustomed to old wine in old wineskins do not take easily to new wine in new wineskins. They are always more comfortable with the old and the familiar.

The problem with the Virgin Birth from the point of view of the biblical narrative is how two entirely different versions of the events surrounding Jesus's birth could have emanated from one source, Mary. The problem disappears if we accept that Mary was not the source of either of these stories. A much more likely scenario than that presented by either Matthew or Luke is that the Virgin Birth was simply not a part of the very early Christian message, and hence Mark's Gospel makes no mention of it. John either knew that it was not a fact or he was unaware of it, suggesting that he wrote in isolation, unaware of some of the beliefs that had come to surround the life of Jesus.

If the Virgin Birth was not a part of the original story, then at some stage, as belief in Jesus as the Son of God crystallised, someone must have realised that he would need to have been born without a human father. This is how almost all of the divine or semi-divine beings in the myths of the ancient world came into existence, the result of some miraculous occurrence generally involving the activities of a supreme male God.

Also, as we shall see later, it is certain that the early Christians searched the scriptures diligently for any possible reference to Jesus. The Greek version of the Isaiah passage would inevitably have come to their attention and would have provided the basis for belief in the Virgin Birth, or confirmation of a belief that had already surfaced. The idea must have become common currency by the time Matthew and Luke wrote their accounts and so both felt the need to include a reference to it. It is very possible that Mary herself was dead by this time, but in any case we have no evidence that she provided any details when she was alive. Thus, both Matthew and Luke would have to invent whatever details they required for their accounts, and if, as seems likely, these were produced independently, without reference to any common source of information, it would explain why they are so completely different: they are simply myth.

The absence of any mention of the Virgin Birth in the letters of St. Paul lends further support to the idea that the Virgin Birth was not a universally known fact in the early Church and that strongly suggests that it was not a fact at all. If that is the case, then it provides worrying evidence that beliefs about Jesus grew over time. The human tendency to exaggerate was not absent from these supposedly sacred writings.

We shall see later on that Luke, while being a very good story-teller, was certainly not a reliable historian. Matthew's accounts of events surrounding the crucifixion and Resurrection also raise the gravest doubts about the reliability of his testimony. And If Jesus was not born to a virgin girl, then any claims made for his divinity must become subject to serious doubt. To claim that it is something that we must "believe by faith", on the grounds that it is a tradition that came to be accepted by our ancient, superstitious ancestors, beggars belief. The Virgin Birth stories furnish evidence that the whole edifice of belief may have been built on foundations of sand. We will find more reason to believe that this might be the case as we examine the issues surrounding the Resurrection and Ascension of Jesus in the next chapter.

3   THE RESURRECTION AND ASCENSION

The Resurrection and Ascension of Jesus are inseparable events in one sense because no Ascension could occur without the Resurrection having occurred. Although the converse is not true, the absence of an Ascension leaves the story somewhat in limbo and certainly does nothing to enhance the case for the Resurrection. What did become of the risen Jesus if he did not ascend into heaven? We will therefore look first at the evidence, or lack of evidence, for the Ascension, because of the two the Ascension has far less biblical support.

Even more than in the case of the Virgin Birth, the Ascension, if it ever occurred, should have become one of the most well-known incidents in the life of Jesus. Unlike the Virgin Birth, where we essentially have to rely on one witness, Mary, who does not even seem to have been responsible for perpetrating the idea, the Ascension would have been witnessed by all of Jesus's disciples. Luke, indeed, tells us that this was the case. It is impossible to imagine that such a unique event, witnessed by at least eleven people and probably more, could ever have been omitted from an account of Jesus's life.

However, in this case, we do not even have accounts written by two separate people when we look at the Gospels and the Acts of the Apostles, the writings specifically detailing the events of Jesus's life and of the early Church. Instead, we have two accounts written by the same person, Luke, one being at the end of his Gospel and the other at the beginning of Acts. Neither Matthew nor Mark (if we discount the added verses 9-20 at the end of his Gospel) makes any mention of it at all. John has Jesus tell Mary Magdalene "*Do not hold on to me, for I have not yet returned to the Father*" (John 20:17) but makes no mention of any actual Ascension event. The fact that three Gospel writers do not specifically mention the event is surely reason enough to doubt that it ever happened.

We even have the problem that Luke's account in his Gospel has significantly different details from those he provides in Acts. In his Gospel, Luke records only two resurrection appearances of Jesus and places both of these on the day on which the Resurrection occurred. He then implies that the Ascension may also have been on that day, although there is some ambiguity at this point.

In Acts, however, Luke states that Jesus appeared to his disciples over a period of forty days and implies a number of appearances, at the end of which time the Ascension occurred. More importantly, Luke's whole story requires all of the followers of Jesus to be in Jerusalem throughout the period between the Resurrection and the Ascension, and the last verse of his Gospel clearly says that they remained there on the instructions of Jesus.

Both Mathew 28:10 and Mark 14:28 contradict Luke's version and say that Jesus promised to appear to the disciples in Galilee. John records three appearances in Jerusalem and then appears to end his Gospel (John 20:30-31), before having second thoughts and adding a final appearance in Galilee, on the shores of Lake Tiberius (the Sea of Galilee). Matthew, in contrast, places the final appearance on a mountain top.

In all this confusion as to the details of these appearances, there is one overriding issue. If Matthew and John were the disciples of Jesus, as is commonly assumed, how is it that neither of them seems to have been aware of the instruction that Luke says Jesus gave to his disciples—to stay in Jerusalem and wait for the promise of the Holy Spirit? This is not a trivial matter. In Luke's narrative he makes it clear that it was central to the whole existence of the early Church. Furthermore, John claims that in one of his resurrection appearances to the disciples, Jesus breathed on them and said "*Receive the Holy Spirit*" (John 20:22). This would appear to be completely at odds with Luke's idea of what happened. Many Christians explain away this anomaly by claiming there is a difference between John's "*receiving the Holy Spirit*" and Luke's being "*baptised with the Holy Spirit*" (Acts 1:5). Others insist that they are one and the same experience. The former view, however, is becoming more and more popular, though the issue is still a very contentious one.

As I have already mentioned, it was the discrepancy between Luke's version and that of the other three Gospel writers that was to provide me with an audacious thought, one that was to change my whole perspective on the Bible narrative. Was it possible that Luke was not trying to write any kind of factual account of what actually happened? Did he, perhaps, have a completely different agenda? Was his overriding concern to write the story of St. Paul and also to explain how the early

Church, the Gentile Church that he had joined and come to know, began its existence?

If this was the case, he would have wanted a story that was simple and yet dramatic. Reality, however, does not always provide simplicity or drama. When it does not, does Luke simply discard it and replace it with an imagined version of events that has both of these attributes? The drama would be contained in two events, an Ascension followed by the coming of the Holy Spirit at Pentecost. These were to be events of such significance and magnitude that, like the crucifixion, they could only occur in Jerusalem. If he had decided to have a biblical, forty day period between the Resurrection and the Ascension, then the Ascension would take place about ten days before the next big Jewish feast, when the disciples might reasonably be expected to return to Jerusalem. Why would they all return any earlier? Obviously, it would be much simpler if they were all to stay in Jerusalem throughout the entire period and hence be on hand for Luke's Ascension story.

If Luke's account of the Ascension event, which has no corroboration from any other source, is indeed fiction, we have no reason to suppose that his account of the day of Pentecost is any different. Indeed, there are compelling reasons for questioning the validity of Luke's account of the drama that he claims occurred on that day, as we shall see in the next chapter.

The accounts of the eight (or possibly nine) resurrection appearances (neglecting those in Mark) are unique to each Gospel, except for the appearance to the disciples on the evening of the Resurrection which is recorded by both Luke and John. The lack of any agreement regarding these appearances indicates that there was no official version of what happened, and this, in turn, suggests that they were not based on fact. In the absence of an agreed version, everybody was free to make up their own stories. It is probable that stories abounded as it is difficult to accept that additions were not made over time. The Resurrection stories do not convey the same degree of certainty that is found in many of the pre-crucifixion narratives. Jesus is presented as a shadowy figure who comes and goes in a seemingly random fashion with no evidence of overall purpose.

Mark's failure to mention any resurrection appearances in the authentic part of his Gospel (ending at Mark 16:8) is very puzzling. It is inconceivable that he would not have included some appearances if he had been aware of any. Somebody clearly realised, at a later date, that this omission was a serious problem and added a further twelve verses to include three appearances, all of which are found in the Gospels of either Luke or John.

If the Gospel accounts of the resurrection appearances are somewhat muddled, they are further complicated by Paul, who, like Luke, was not an eye-witness to any of this. He declares that Jesus first appeared to Peter (no women involved here!), then to the Twelve (although there were only eleven by this stage—was Paul not aware of Judas having committed suicide?) then to *more than five hundred brothers at the same time,* then to James, then to all the apostles and last of all to Paul himself (1Corinthians 15:5-8).

More than five hundred of the brothers at one time? When on earth could this have occurred? In the first place, there would have had to be more than five hundred brothers assembled together. Who organised such a gathering and why? How could they gather without drawing attention to themselves? And exactly what was the object of appearing to this large number, when the purposes of Jesus seemed to have been entrusted to a very small group? Luke says in Acts 1:15 that after the Ascension, Peter stood up among the believers, a group, including women, that numbered about a hundred and twenty. It is hard to accept that if more than five hundred brothers had seen the resurrected Jesus at one time, only 120 people (including the women presumably) would have remained in Jerusalem waiting for the promise of the Holy Spirit.

We cannot be certain from which sources Luke or Paul obtained their information. Paul certainly met the apostles, though why they would have provided him with information that was not mentioned in the Gospels is hard to explain. It does seem very strange that none of the Gospel writers remember, or were aware of, any appearance involving more than five hundred brothers.

Luke's claim in Acts (as opposed to his Gospel account) that Jesus's appearances occurred over a period of forty days, meaning perhaps a protracted period, raises more problems. During this time we are told that Jesus "*spoke* [to them] *about the kingdom of God*" (Acts 1:3). However, on the day of the Ascension, the disciples ask him, "*Lord, are you at this time going to restore the kingdom to Israel*?" Jesus's reply is ambiguous but does not attempt to squash the idea. He simply says that the timing of certain events is a secret known only by the Father (Acts 1:7). This suggests that Jesus, neither in his normal lifetime, nor after the Resurrection, had managed to get his message across to them, or else it implies that this must have formed an integral part of his message.

Then, the disciples were all Galileans, visitors to Jerusalem for the feast of the Passover. They could not have made any prior preparations for an extended stay in the city or the surrounding area as they could hardly have expected to be overtaken by such drastic circumstances. Galileans, more than most other outsiders, were probably tolerated rather than welcomed in Jerusalem and it is highly unlikely that this toleration would have extended to include overstaying their welcome. People from Nazareth seemed to have had a particularly bad reputation (John 1:46). Luke, however, requires us to accept that at least one hundred and twenty of Jesus's Galilean followers stayed on indefinitely after the Passover feast had ended. In the grand scheme of his account, he conveniently fails to mention the mundane matters of practical daily living. How did these people feed themselves?

Are we to conclude that Jerusalem was a sufficiently large city that so many up-country strangers could melt away into its shadows almost without trace? There are references to barred doors due to a fear of the Jews (John 20:19). This does not suggest they were living like gypsies in makeshift shelters outside the city walls. Did they really just forget all about their homes in Galilee? The whole idea poses problems that, again, are by no means trivial. What a pity Luke provides us with such scant information, because if more had been included, it could have lent considerably more credibility to the whole story.

What is much more likely is that all the followers of Jesus returned to Galilee, as reported by three of the Gospel writers, and that they stayed there. It seems most improbable that they would have wished to make a return to Jerusalem for a significant period of time, long enough at least for the passions that would have been aroused by the events of the crucifixion to subside, particularly so if the Jews of Jerusalem had indeed been complicit in the execution of their Galilean leader. They would have had every reason to fear for their safety in Jerusalem.

The authorities on the other hand, Jewish and Roman, would have had every reason to be extremely vigilant, fearful of a possible influx of inflamed Galileans so soon after such a traumatic event. It is not believable that the close followers of Jesus would have turned up in any numbers for the very next Jewish festival, Shavuot (Pentecost), fifty days later, a day that is critical to the whole of Luke's account of the early Church.

Last of all, it is very difficult to imagine what Jesus could have been doing over such a protracted period of forty days. He was not with his Father, because he had not yet ascended. He was not with his disciples for most of the time as less than a dozen appearances are specifically mentioned, most of them seemingly quite brief. He does not seem to have been overly worried about correcting the misconceptions they appeared to hold. He had no further ministry on the Earth to prepare for. He does not seem to have been writing his memoirs. He could not simply cease to exist between appearances. The thought of a disembodied spirit floating around in no-man's-land for such a protracted period of time with little apparent purpose in mind is a rather difficult concept to cope with and a rather unlikely scenario. How could the disciples have ended up being so confused as to the real purpose of Jesus life and death? Why did Jesus not spend a lot more time with them and clear up their misconceptions? Could the answer be that dreams tend to be rather intermittent affairs? We will return to this point later on.

Muddled, unconvincing and conflicting as a lot of the information is, there is a further issue which throws yet more doubt upon the Resurrection. This focuses on the crucial events of the day of Pentecost as described by Luke, and it is sufficiently important to merit a separate chapter of its own.

It is unfortunate that only one account exists of the activities of the very early Church, that is, the period from the crucifixion/Resurrection/Ascension of Jesus to the appearance of Paul on the scene. This account is provided by Luke, a person of whom we have practically no knowledge. It is highly questionable to assume that he was intimately acquainted with any of the people that he writes about or that he had any direct knowledge of a number of the events that he describes. The version that he gives of the events following Paul's conversion, for example, is totally at odds with Paul's own account in Galatians 1:13-24, suggesting that he was certainly not acquainted with this letter and that, very possibly, any personal acquaintance with Paul that he may have had was not a particularly intimate one. This despite his obvious interest in the life of Paul, the "we" passage in Acts chapter 16, the "us" in Acts 21:18 and even Paul's reference to "*Our dear friend Luke*" in Colossians 4:14.

The problem raised by Luke's account of the events at Pentecost first surfaces in Acts chapter 6 when we are introduced to a man called Stephen. Stephen was one of seven people appointed to help with the practical, day to day organisation of the Church community and so set the apostles free to attend to the more important work of prayer and preaching the Word of God. Stephen, however, turned out to be far more than just a practical administrator. He was a very gifted preacher in his own right and he "*did great wonders and miraculous signs among the people*" (Acts 6:8). It was Stephen's forthright preaching that was to precipitate the first major crisis in the early Church and, indeed, his own death.

Stephen was a Jew and he offended the Jews of one particular synagogue in Jerusalem to the extent that they dragged him before the Sanhedrin, the supreme Jewish authority in civil and religious affairs, essentially accusing him of saying that the new Jesus movement would eventually **replace** Judaism. Chapter 7 of Acts records Stephen's defence in which he summarises the history of the Jews, making it plain that they had never been an obedient people and that this disobedience had finally culminated in the murder of Jesus, God's anointed Messiah. There is no mention of the Resurrection, but Stephen claims to see a vision of Jesus standing at the right hand of God. At this point, he is dragged outside the city and stoned to death.

The stoning of Stephen reveals just how volatile the Jews of the day were. Their passions were easily inflamed into murderous rage when their religion was attacked. We have a parallel situation to this in our own day. When Salman Rushdie attacked the prophet Muhammad in his 1988 novel, *The Satanic Verses*, thousands of incensed Muslims took to the streets in fury, demanding the death of the infidel. These people were not extremists or terrorists, but ordinary citizens of Britain, provoked to such anger for one reason only—their religion had been attacked. They were not even in the presence of Mr Rushdie. One shudders to think what might have happened to Mr Rushdie if he had been within their reach. When we realise just how extremely sensitive people can be when it comes to the matter of their religious beliefs, we are confronted with the problem of why these volatile Jews should have stoned Stephen but not Peter or any of the other apostles.

When Paul returns to Jerusalem for the last time, at the end of his third missionary journey, he is recognised by some Jews who react in a similar manner to the way they, or others, had reacted to Stephen, shouting "*Men of Israel, help us! This is the man who teaches all men everywhere against our people and our law and this place* [the temple]" (Acts 21:28). They were only prevented from killing him because news of the uproar reached the Roman troops stationed in the city. All the while, James [presumably Jesus's brother] and the elders of the church in Jerusalem are comfortably coexisting alongside these same Jews. Indeed, they boasted to Paul of how many thousands of Jews had believed and that all of them were "*zealous for the law*" (Acts 21:20).

No Christian today is zealous for the law. The law is associated with the Old Covenant. Christians today understand that they live under the New Covenant, by grace. The two things are not compatible, as Paul was well aware. The Jerusalem Church contained people who actually knew Jesus during his lifetime and yet their idea of Christianity could not possibly have been consistent with today's version or even with Paul's version. Today's version of Christianity is the Pauline version, not the Jewish version, whatever that might have been.

According to Luke, on the day of Pentecost, Peter had preached a similar message to that of Stephen, making it quite plain that his hearers were responsible for the death of Jesus, "*a man accredited by God*" (Acts 2:22). However, he then goes much further than Stephen and we should note carefully the following three statements that he makes. First: "*God has raised this Jesus to life, and we are all witnesses of the fact*" (v 32). He later explains the significance of this event in a second statement: "*Therefore let all the house of Israel be assured of this: God has made this Jesus, whom you crucified, both Lord and Christ*" (v 36). The required response, furthermore, is contained in the third statement, that they should "*Repent and be baptised, every one of you, in the name of Jesus Christ for the forgiveness of your sins*" (v 38).

These statements would appear to be more inflammatory than anything Stephen said and clearly suggest that Judaism had been rendered obsolete with immediate effect. There would appear to be no further requirement for obedience to the Law of Moses or for temple sacrifices. Such statements represent the introduction of the New Covenant and are in line with a modern understanding of the Gospel. No Jew could possibly have thought that this new teaching was compatible with what he already believed.

Why, therefore, was the response to Peter's message so very different to that provoked by Stephen? How did a bunch of despised Galileans, easily identifiable by their accents, remain in Jerusalem and preach these seditious ideas among such a volatile people and still live to tell the tale? Why did the authorities, who showed few qualms over getting rid of the leader, then hesitate to take effective action against his close Galilean followers? It makes no sense.

There is only one explanation that does make any sense to me and that is that no message such as the one that Luke attributes to Peter on the day of Pentecost was, in fact, ever preached. There simply could not have been any proclamation, in Jerusalem, of a physical resurrection with all the implications that this would entail. No message making the Jews culpable for the murder of God's Messiah would have been tolerated. Luke invented all of this because it provided a very simple, neat explanation of the existence of the early Church. The events of this day were what transformed the disciples understanding of the real significance of Jesus's life and changed them as people, turning them into a group of self-confident, miracle-working evangelists.

If the major discrepancy between Luke's account, and the other accounts, of the events following the Resurrection is due to the fact that Luke has invented his material for a specific reason, we have to ask why he feels free to do this. The obvious answer is that no "official" version of the events following the crucifixion (or supposed Resurrection) existed. Rumour, supposition and possibly dreams were all that anybody had to go on because no actual resurrection appearances took place.

A more likely scenario than the one described by Luke, is that the Jesus movement began to grow in Galilee and continued as a sect within Judaism for a considerable period of time before the disciples felt confident enough to go back to Jerusalem. According to Luke, the temple continued to be a focus for the apostles' worship (Acts 3:1), but this is unlikely to have been the case as early as he imagines that it was. It simply serves to emphasise that the movement, when it returned to Jerusalem, continued as some sort of reformed Jewish sect, one which emphasised the idea of the kingdom of God on earth.

The first clear mention of a Gentile, or non-Jewish, convert occurs in Acts chapter 10 with the story of Cornelius. This appears as a very isolated incident, but it may have been inserted here because of the important bearing that it was to have on the decision of the Council of Jerusalem regarding the issue of circumcision (Acts 15). The first mention of a serious attempt to evangelise the Gentiles is possibly in Acts 11:20, although even here it is not made clear if Gentile converts were expected to become converts to Judaism and accept circumcision.

The first definitely non-Jewish, uncircumcised converts of whom we can be certain did not appear until Paul's first missionary journey, when there was clearly a significant influx of them into the fellowship. It was this event that triggered the crisis meeting in Jerusalem where it was decided that circumcision would not be maintained as a requirement for the Gentile believers, a decision that would ultimately allow Christianity to become a world religion.

Up to this point, it must have been the case that circumcision was assumed and hence the movement had to be a totally Jewish one. It was this momentous decision that was also responsible for causing the first fissure in the early Church, with two strands of the faith seemingly being approved—a Jewish strand and a Pauline, Gentile strand. It would take many more years for the fissure to run its inevitable course and cause a complete separation between the new and the old, with the old eventually disappearing. In all likelihood, however, the split was not finalised until after the catastrophic Jewish revolt against the Romans that, in 70 CE, resulted in significant destruction of the city of Jerusalem together with a total destruction of the temple and heralded both the end of traditional Judaism and the emergence of a new, transformed, synagogue-based Judaism.

If we infer that the early Church must have conducted itself in a way that allowed it to avoid a major confrontation with Judaism, why does Luke tell of events on the day of Pentecost that would, under such circumstances, seem to be so highly unlikely? The answer probably lies in the fact that neither Luke nor his readers had the advantage of a modern, western, university education. The anomalies in his account may cause some of us to raise our eyebrows today but they clearly did not trouble Luke or his readers. Indeed, they do not seem to trouble the vast majority of present day believers.

It is difficult to avoid the impression that Luke's main interest lay with the life of St. Paul, the man largely responsible for the Church with which Luke was familiar. The first few chapters of Acts form a bridge between the termination of Jesus's life on earth and the appearance of St. Paul on the scene. The end of one era, Jesus's presence on the earth, and the beginning of the next, the birth of the Jesus movement under the leadership of Peter, are marked by dramatic events, the tool of any good story-teller. The events of Pentecost are followed by accounts of great miracles and further manifestations of the Spirit that add interest to the whole story but were probably based on folklore. Luke was very fond of the supernatural and not over-concerned, it seems, about factual accuracy.

It is easy for us, living in an era of considerable economic prosperity and with the leisure time that accompanies this, armed with an entire New Testament easily to hand and all the modern facilities for study, to stand back and try to take a more objective look at the whole picture to see how it all fits together. Luke did not have any of these advantages. What he did have was a very important story to tell, and in his day that would have been a sufficiently monumental task without any unnecessary complications. He could be forgiven for imagining that the message he first heard was the message that had always been preached. The idea that there might have been any development of this message, or that the scenario he creates at Pentecost would have been highly unlikely, would not have occurred to him, particularly if he was not a Jew. Why should it? Such ideas may be of academic interest in our day but Luke was not interested in academic matters. He simply places ideas that were current at the time he was writing in a much earlier period, seven weeks after the crucifixion, at the next Jewish feast to occur after the Passover, the festival of Shavuot or Pentecost.

From the point of view of a writer with Luke's agenda, the account of the day of Pentecost is a masterpiece. It has great drama and provides a compelling account of the beginning of the early Church, an event precipitated by the outpouring of the Holy Spirit as promised, according to Luke, by Jesus. (Luke 24:49; Acts 1:8). This is why it all started. It also explains the phenomenon of speaking with tongues, something which had clearly become a prominent feature within the early Church by the time Luke was writing. Paul makes reference to it (1 Corinthians 14).

The coming of the Spirit not only miraculously cleared up all the confusion and misconceptions of the disciples, but it infused such a feeling of enthusiasm and power in them that they simply could not remain silent. We are told that they began to "*speak in other tongues*" and proclaimed the wonders of God in many different languages (Acts 2:6). This provides a convenient introduction to Peter's first sermon, which begins by explaining to the startled onlookers that what was actually happening was a fulfilment of an Old Testament prophecy found in Joel 2:28-32, and it serves to authenticate the message that Peter continues with, namely the message of the New Covenant, sealed with the blood of the crucified and now risen Jesus.

The detail about many onlookers hearing the wonders of God proclaimed in their own language is one we might expect to find in an account penned by someone of Luke's gift for story-telling and his ability to capture his reader's attention by introducing a supernatural element. In Luke's day there is little doubt that supernatural events would have added to the credibility and the wonder of it all. Finally, it explains the origin of the supposed miracle working power that the apostles apparently became endowed with. Exaggerated rumours of what they supposedly did would have become embedded in the folklore of the early believers and Luke found a way of explaining it all.

Unfortunately, in the cold light of day, the events described are so unlikely that we must assume that they are no more than another figment of Luke's vivid imagination, just as his account of the Incarnation must have been. If this is the case, we have to ask just how much of what Luke wrote can really be trusted. Is his Gospel also riddled with other unreliable information? Indeed, is Luke likely to have been any different from the other Gospel writers? Are any of the accounts that we have reliable enough to base so much of our belief system on them?

Human beings, of course, like simplicity. We want things that are easy to understand. And, unfortunately, we are prone to accept what is straightforward, even if false, in preference to some more complicated truth, particularly if the straightforward version is one that we would like to believe in. The fact that no other Gospel writer offers any corroboration of Luke's account clearly marks it as a most unreliable source of evidence. The possibility that there was no day of Pentecost as Luke describes it would, of course, carry very serious implications for two of the most successful branches of the Christian Church today: the Pentecostals and all the charismatic groups.

There is the suggestion that a similar simplification may have occurred with Luke's account of Jesus's appearance to two travellers on the road to Emmaus, when he uses the Scriptures to explain the whole purpose of his crucifixion (Luke 24:25-27). Luke is conveying the fact that Jesus was seen to be the Christ only through a proper understanding of the Scriptures. We know that Paul had a reputation for "*proving from the Scriptures that Jesus was the Christ*" (Acts 18:28). Is it possible that Jesus's disciples, over time, came to understand the meaning of his life and death from a study of the Scriptures and that Luke simply found it easier, from the point of view of his narrative, to compress this whole process into two events, the appearances that he records taking place on the day of the Resurrection?

For our purposes at the moment, it is sufficient to note that if no such event as Pentecost took place, then there would have been no sudden proclamation in Jerusalem of the Resurrection, a fact which reduces the possibility that the new movement began life in Jerusalem as Luke would have us believe. Everything would make a lot more sense if we were to assume that it started somewhere in Galilee. This would have avoided confrontation with the Jerusalem authorities, and if significant time elapsed before the disciples ever returned to Jerusalem, any problems regarding the possible whereabouts of Jesus's body would have been lost in the mists of time. It would have been quite impossible for anyone to produce a body that could have been identified as that of Jesus

A Galilean movement could easily have spread north to places such as Damascus, where Paul almost certainly first encountered it, more easily than to Jerusalem in the south. If this was the case, it would avoid the need to explain the thorny problem of why Paul should have decided to go one hundred and thirty five miles from Jerusalem to Damascus, a Syrian city, in search of members of this new sect to arrest. Surely there were plenty of these people more conveniently placed, nearer to hand? Why would Paul have expected to find members of this sect specifically in Damascus?

We are still left, however, with the problem of explaining how belief in a physically resurrected Jesus came into being, and we shall address this problem at some length in a later chapter.

There is one last issue that needs a mention. Peter quotes the prophet Joel to explain the unusual behaviour of the gathered assembly on the day of Pentecost. However, he says that this is specifically a prophecy for the "last days" (Acts 2:17). Peter, of course, thought that he was living in the last days. If Peter was inspired by the Holy Spirit, why are we all still here two thousand years later?

5   THE MIRACLES AND THE
TRANSFIGURATION

The reported miraculous ministry of Jesus poses problems from more than one point of view. I have heard it said, more than once, that in response to any situation, the Christian should always ask himself (or herself) *"What would Jesus have done?"* The answer, in most cases, is that Jesus would have healed the sick person, given back the blind person their sight, made the deaf to hear and the lame to walk. An answer, in other words, that is completely irrelevant to me, for I am not able to do any of these things in spite of reading the works of people who were, or still are, famous for their healing ministries, people such as Smith-Wigglesworth, T.L. Osborn and more recently Benny Hinn, but there are also many others.

T.L.Osborn was active in Kenya while I was teaching in Uganda and on one occasion I passed through a Kenyan town at a time when he was conducting a crusade there. I had not really heard of him at that time but I was soon to discover how successful his ministry had been and how much influence he exerted. Many of the friends that I was to make had been converted under his preaching and were avid followers of his teachings. I heard many of the tape-recorded messages from his African crusades and I too became very attracted to his ideas. However, I cannot comment on the claims which he makes for the healings and miracles that he says are regular features of his crusades, except to note that they must, at the very least, be exaggerated.

This is not to say that I myself have never prayed for the sick or seen the sick quickly recover afterwards. It is simply to say that nobody immediately rose from a sickbed as a result of my prayers and certainly nobody ever received their sight or hearing and the lame never walked. If I am unable to do the works that Jesus did, I have to ask myself, what use is the example of Jesus to me? Nothing that I can do is what Jesus would have done in most situations. This feeling of helplessness I found difficult to cope with. Maybe if Jesus had been a more ordinary person he would have been more relevant to my life. There was always a gap between what I believed with my head and what I actually experienced in reality. I found it little help to be told that one day, when I got to heaven, everything would be made plain. Then I would understand. Then, of course, it would be too late to be of any use.

Shortly after my elder son turned thirteen, he began to suffer from nose bleeds. These did not concern us at first but as they persisted and became increasingly difficult to stop, we were obliged to take him to the doctor. A scan was ordered and this was to reveal some rather bad news. Our son had a growth called an angiofibroma and would need major surgery to remove it. The hospital had not seen a case of this that anyone could remember and nursing staff were apparently given special training in how to care for our son after the operation, assuming that he survived the procedure.

Before the operation, he had to undergo a preliminary operation in which a catheter was fed into his groin and then manoeuvred up to the base of the skull and into an artery that was feeding the tumorous growth that was somewhere inside his head, so that a plug could be introduced to cut off the blood supply. After this initial operation was finished, we were taken into a room and shown a recorded imaging of it. On a screen we saw a large, black, pulsating mass and then we watched in astonishment as the pulsations stopped when the plug was inserted. To our enormous relief, the procedure had been completely successful. I could only marvel that the medical profession was capable of such an extraordinary feat.

Within a week, the operation to remove the growth was performed. We were told that it could take anything up to eight hours but in the event he was out of the theatre in about five and a half hours, albeit five and a half agonising hours for us. He was taken to the intensive care room but we could not see him for a while as we were told that one of his lungs had collapsed and that doctors were with him. He survived and we were allowed to stay with him overnight. Full recovery took about three months as we had to take him to the hospital every week to change the bandages that were packed into his nose to stop bleeding occurring.

Throughout this entire episode, I was conscious that my faith was in the medical profession, not in the power of prayer. Of course we prayed, but we prayed for a successful outcome to the operation. My head told me that healing should have been possible through faith alone, but I was certainly not prepared to risk the life of my son on the strength of my faith. I was determined to take every advantage of the progress of modern science. Without these operations my son would simply have died. I obviously needed to bring my faith in line with my head knowledge or I needed to modify my head knowledge to bring it in line with what I clearly believed when the chips were down.

There are two particular recorded miracles of Jesus that caused me major concern. The first is the raising of Lazarus from the dead, as told in St. John's Gospel chapter 11. Jesus had been to the place where John the Baptist had his early ministry and may still have been there when he received a message that Lazarus was sick. We are clearly told that the disciples of Jesus were with him when he received the message and that Jesus deliberately delayed going to the aid of his friend. When he did go, taking his disciples with him, he arrived four days after Lazarus had been buried. Nevertheless, Jesus orders the stone to be removed from the cave where Lazarus had been laid. One of the sisters of Lazarus protests, saying that by now the decaying body would have started to smell. Jesus, however, asks for faith, promising that those who believed "*would see the glory of God*" (John 11:40). On Jesus's orders, the stone is then removed and Lazarus is instructed to come forth. He does so under his own steam, although still somewhat hampered by the burial cloths. Once these have been removed, Lazarus is fully back in the world of the living.

Of all the miracles that Jesus is said to have performed during his lifetime, this surely must rank as the greatest. True, there are two other instances where Jesus is said to have brought people back to life, but in both cases the death had been recent. Lazarus was raised after four days lying in the in the tomb, after four days of bodily decay in a hot climate. Even if he had still been alive when buried, he would have been totally dehydrated and in no fit state to make it to the cave entrance under his own steam after his resuscitation.

So the question arises as to why nobody else seems to remember this awesome miracle? Why is the miracle not recorded in any other Gospel? Could it be that by the time John wrote his Gospel, it would have been very unlikely that any witnesses were left alive and that there would be nobody around to dispute the account? It is commonly accepted that John's Gospel was the last to be compiled and indeed, we cannot be certain that it was John the disciple who wrote this Gospel.

If any of the other Gospel writers had been familiar with John's Gospel, or had been witnesses to this event, how is it possible that they would not think to mention it? John makes it clear that the disciples (presumably all, not just some) were there, no doubt with many mourners. Are we being asked to believe that they just forgot about it? Or that they thought the miracle was not sufficiently special or important to warrant any mention? Or perhaps Matthew's Gospel was not actually written by Matthew the disciple after all?

The most likely explanation, I suspect, is that John invented this miracle in order to drive home the message that Jesus must have delivered at some stage in his ministry, namely what is recorded in verse 25 of this story: "*I am the resurrection and the life; he who believes in me, though he die, yet shall he live, and whoever lives and believes in me shall never die*" (RSV).

The second recorded miracle of Jesus that gave me cause for concern is found in John 9:1-12, where we read about the healing of a man who had been born blind. Interestingly, in verse 1, Jesus's disciples betray the superstitions beliefs of the age: if a man is born blind, then somebody must have sinned to cause this. The image of God that this belief portrays hardly does God or the disciples much credit. Jesus challenges this superstitious notion and proceeds to heal the man concerned, although the healing is a little unusual, the man being told to go and wash in the Pool of Siloam in order to receive his sight.

When my younger son was seven years old, a routine eye test at his school revealed one eye to be very weak. We were told to take him to an optician who prescribed spectacles. However, whenever my son put these on, he complained of seeing two of everything—the spectacles gave him double vision. The optician told us that, unfortunately, the condition had probably been diagnosed too late. For there to have been a realistic chance of the problem being corrected, diagnosis by the age of five was really necessary. It seems probable that our son missed a routine eye test through absence from school and this was never chased up, possibly due to the government cuts that were in operation at the time, during the Thatcher years. Nothing much seems to have changed judging by our present predicament.

We see with the brain and not with our eyes, however essential the eyes may be to vision. It is the eyes that must receive the optical signals, but the brain has to learn to make sense of these signals and produce an image from them. In most people, the brain learns to synthesise the two slightly separate images from each eye to form one image. However, it sometimes happens that when one eye is much weaker than the other, the brain will ignore the signal from the weaker eye and simply use the signal from the stronger eye. When it does this, it does not need to synthesise two signals and therefore never learns to do so. After a certain age, the brain becomes "hard-wired" and from then on a proper synthesis of two signals becomes impossible.

This raises the question, if a man is born blind so that the brain has never learned to process any optical signal at all from the eyes, what sense would it be able to make of two signals suddenly being received if his eyes were to be "opened"? To someone like St John, who would know nothing of the part that the brain plays in vision, the "opening" of a man's eyes would automatically result in the ability to see. Modern science does not agree. In the very rare cases where someone has had their sight "restored" in adulthood, having lost their sight at some early stage of life, there are huge problems with optical-spatial awareness, the ability to appreciate distance and see in three dimensions. Such are the problems associated with this that correcting eye defects in people who have been blind from an early age, even where this is now a theoretical possibility, is not necessarily a recommended procedure.

This supposed miracle of Jesus is one that suddenly takes on enormous proportions, no longer just a matter of opening the eyes but also of configuring the brain to cope with the received signals. It is akin to God creating two human beings in the Garden of Eden with ready-made language ability. To me John's story is not one that inspires much confidence in its being based in historical fact. Might it not be just a case of another invented story, this time to illustrate another great theme of Jesus's teaching, found in verse 5, namely *"I am the light of the world,"* and also to reinforce the teaching that it is Jesus who is able to bring spiritual enlightenment to the spiritually blind?

To accept this explanation, however, only raises another unanswerable question once again: if either of these miracles was invented, where does the factual material in any account end and the illustrative story part start? It also inevitably leads to the question of whether Jesus performed any major miracles at all. And there is no simple answer. This is why, for those wishing to believe in a divinely inspired Bible, it is so much easier to accept all of it as being inerrant fact, however improbable these facts may appear to be, on the grounds that *"nothing is impossible with God"* (Luke 1:37). This neatly side-steps all the problems associated with a Bible that might be part fact and part religious myth, although all divinely inspired, except for the ever increasing amount of faith needed to keep on top of all the things that have to be believed by faith.

There is a further issue with many of the healings that Jesus performed, as they were apparently achieved through the casting out of demons from the afflicted person. Jesus, therefore, must have accepted the common belief of his time that demons were a major cause of illness. It is very difficult to justify such beliefs in the twenty-first century, despite the revival of interest shown in these matters, including interest by the established churches. Anyone who has witnessed exorcists at work (there have been a number of television documentary programmes about exorcists over the years) would not know whether to laugh or cry. They are ludicrous in the extreme and sadly there is evidence of considerable harm but very little good resulting from these procedures, practised by utter exhibitionists whose mental stability appears to be seriously in doubt. Jesus never needed to indulge in such theatrics as his word alone carried sufficient authority to force obedience from demons. However, it does suggest that he was a man limited by the knowledge of his time and this must have some bearing on a belief that views him as the Son of God. Is it possible to accept that any serious healings could have been achieved by such dubious means?

One more miraculous event that must be mentioned is the Transfiguration, which is recorded in all three synoptic Gospels and is mentioned in Peter's second letter. This is in a different category because it is not a miracle actually performed by Jesus, although it does require us to believe that he knew in advance that the event was going to take place. Jesus had taken Peter, James and John to a mountain top, where his appearance became radiant and the two greatest figures of the Old Testament, Moses, the law-giver and Elijah, the prophet, appeared to him and talked with him. The voice of God is then heard, telling the three disciples that Jesus is his Son (and therefore greater than Moses or Elijah) and they should listen to him.

There is one major problem in all this. John was one of those present at this event but there is no mention of this incident in the Gospel of John. John's Gospel is devoted entirely to the theme of Jesus being the Son of God. Why would he, once again, neglect to include an incident which, along with the Virgin Birth, provides such unequivocal support for the idea of Jesus's unique status? This was a major event his life, equivalent to his Ascension. It was well known. How could any Gospel fail to mention it? If the Gospel of John was written by the disciple, it casts great doubt over the authenticity of the story. If the reason for the omission is that the writer is not the disciple and knew nothing of it, then we are faced with the problem that none of the Gospel writers may have been among the followers of Jesus and we could be left with only a tenuous connection between the life of Jesus and the written accounts of that life.

One possible explanation of this event is that it was a story invented by Peter, James and John to claim pre-eminence in the early days of the new movement. We know that James and John were ambitious from the story recorded in Mark 10:35-37, where they ask to be allowed to sit on either side of Jesus when he enters his glory, perhaps meaning when the kingdom of God (on earth) is established. Peter seems to have become the natural leader after the death of Jesus, with John his right-hand man. One does wonder why Jesus would have chosen just three disciples to witness this event, just as we must wonder why half of the disciples are never mentioned again after the Ascension. It is a story that the other disciples could not dispute but one which must have been a potential cause for jealousy and division amongst them.

We can now appreciate that each of the four facets of Jesus's life that have been discussed are riddled with uncertainties, improbabilities and inconsistencies. There is a high probability that there was no Virgin Birth and no Ascension. The Resurrection must be classified as an event lacking convincing proof and the accounts of the some of the miracles very suspect. The Transfiguration is another event of such magnitude that, if true, should have appeared in every Gospel. It does not, and more importantly, it is missing from the one Gospel supposedly written by someone who was present at the event. The overall result is that very little confidence can be put in the most crucial issues relating to Christian belief, leaving the possibility that the entire edifice may well be constructed not just on sand but on quicksand. However, this is only the beginning. There are equally serious question marks over a number of other issues and we shall look at some of these in the following chapters.

6 THE CONVERSION OF SAUL (ST. PAUL)

The conversion of St. Paul presents a huge problem if there is any truth in Paul's claim that it occurred as a direct intervention from the risen Jesus. The Jesus of the Gospels appeared to glory in the fact that God (his Father) had "*hidden these things from the wise and learned, and revealed them to little children,*" his uneducated disciples, no doubt, being foremost in his mind (Matthew 11:25; Luke 10:21). Paul's conversion would imply that the risen and ascended Jesus had had a change of mind. Paul belonged to the educated, elite class, and it now appears that Jesus is side-lining his original disciples in favour of someone of quite different ilk.

Spending some considerable time as his personal disciples and receiving the promised baptism with the Holy Spirit at Pentecost are, apparently, no longer deemed sufficient to carry out the purposes that Jesus now has in mind, for Paul's conversion represents a seismic shift in the history of the movement. From now on, the purposes of God would seem to be entrusted primarily to this newcomer. It is Paul who will turn the Church from being a Jewish sect into what was to become, ultimately, a near universal organisation.

We have already noted that the accounts of the Resurrection are a hopeless muddle. It turns out that the accounts of Paul's conversion are every bit as bad. The most well-known of these accounts is the one that Luke gives us in Acts chapter 9. Saul (Paul), while on a journey to Damascus to arrest any Jewish Christians he could find there, is struck blind by a flash of light from heaven and hears the voice of Jesus. He then has to be led by others for the remainder of the journey to a place where he meets Ananias and receives back his sight. Immediately, we are told, he begins preaching that Jesus is the Christ. This so upsets the Jews of Damascus that he has to flee for his life and he goes to Jerusalem, where he is introduced to the apostles by a man called Barnabas. He spends some time with them and preaches there before being sent off to the city of Tarsus for his own safety.

This version is more or less repeated in Acts 22:6-17, on the occasion of Paul's defence before the crowd in Jerusalem. This time, the words are put into Paul's own mouth, but the writer (Luke) does give the impression of having been an eyewitness to this event. This would seem to be highly unlikely because Paul's own version of the events following his conversion is significantly different from what Luke tells us.

Luke then says that Paul made a second visit to Jerusalem before embarking on his first missionary journey. On this occasion he was accompanied by Barnabas and the purpose was to take gifts from the Church at Antioch to the Church at Jerusalem during a time of famine (Acts 11:30). A third visit occurs after his first missionary journey, when the issue of circumcision had become a problem following significant numbers of Gentile converts into the Church (Acts 15).

Some time elapsed after Paul's conversion and before he began his first missionary journey. It is possible that Paul's understanding of the Gospel was beginning to change because near the start of this journey he decides to be known by one of his other names, Paul, and he ceases to be known as Saul from this time on. Name changes can often be used to mark a significant change in someone's life. We do not know why the name change was made in this case, but could it be that Paul had come to realise that his new religion superseded Judaism and rendered the latter obsolete?

There is no doubt that Paul's conversion would have put him in a very difficult position, one with which I can fully empathise. At some stage in my own journey, I must have crossed the line separating the grey area of doubt from that of unbelief. I do not know exactly when this occurred. It was not a sudden event as Paul's conversion seems to have been. Rather, it was result of a constant drip of negative experiences. Foremost among these were the radio programmes that, as a result of my being retired, my wife was able to call me to come and listen to. She abhors silence and so either the radio or the television will be on whenever we are at home. I received "the call" whenever there was a discussion programme involving the issue of homosexuality, and there seemed to be a number of these.

There would invariably be some spokesperson from a Christian organisation on the panel, or who phoned in, putting the "Christian viewpoint". The more I heard, the angrier I became. Many of these contributions were made by people whose self-righteousness, bigotry and ignorance were matched only by their arrogant assumption that to uphold the Bible position on this, and indeed all other issues, put them on a higher moral plane than everybody else. The implication was that they were seeking to uphold the moral values approved by God and on which this nation had been built, in contrast to others who only sought to destroy such values. Gradually, I realised that I no longer wished to be associated in any way with these people or their views, and I slowly reached the point where I was more than happy to declare myself to be on the opposite side of the fence altogether. It was around this time that I finally accepted that my journey had now reached the point of no return. I think that secretly, although I had already crossed the line, I harboured the hope that I might, by some miracle, be able to cross back again, that God would yet rescue me from this bleak world that I had entered.

The dilemma I faced after taking this decisive step was that of how to tell everybody else of my "conversion" from faith to unbelief. It is by no means an easy matter and it is one that I still have not completely resolved. Perhaps that is part of the reason that I am writing this book. Not only has it helped me to clarify my own thoughts and beliefs, to be sure of exactly where I now stand, but, if this ever sees print, I will be able to give copies to those with whom I was once friendly and who perhaps might like to know what became of me.

That certainly seems a more attractive option than trying to explain my total change of mind in person. The risks of this procedure are too great. Who can say how such news would be received? It will be better to give people some time to digest and then come to terms with my decision, unless I have already been consigned to history. How much easier it would be to deal with if it had occurred as the result of one dramatic incident rather than being the result of a complicated, long drawn-out process.

Paul's position would have been no less difficult. How could he explain such a complete about-turn on an issue of such monumental importance without losing all credibility? Maybe that was his whole purpose in retreating to Arabia (Galatians 1:17), away from all those who knew him, to lie low and consider how best to proceed. First he would need to be very clear about what his new beliefs were and how he could justify them. He would need time to clarify his thoughts, time to study and think. But one thing probably became clear to him. Explanations could, in large measure, be avoided if he claimed that it was the result of a direct intervention from the risen Jesus himself.

When Paul talks about his conversion in Galatians 1:15-18, he makes exactly this claim without supplying any details. We can gather that he was in, or near, Damascus (v 17). There is no mention of his having been in Jerusalem and making the journey to Damascus for the specific purpose of arresting members of this new sect. It seems more likely that Paul was resident in Damascus when this new sect spread to that city and that he was violently opposed to it, but later changed his mind.

He tells us that he received his Gospel directly from the risen Jesus in a revelation, but again he does not say what this entailed. However, the significance of this claim is enormous. Not only does it supply Paul with a way out of his dilemma, of explaining his astonishing change of mind, but it also has the advantage of immediately putting him on an equal footing with all of the original apostles, for whom, incidentally, he appears to have had scant regard. He refers to Peter, John and James (presumably Jesus's brother as James the brother of John had already been killed [Acts 12:2]) with the somewhat unflattering statement, "*those **reputed** to be pillars*" (Galatians 2:9 [emphasis added]), and he insisted (v 6) that they had added nothing to his message.

The apostles, in turn, would find it difficult to refute Paul's claim. Revelation is generally something that is given to an individual and rarely, if ever, are there other witnesses. This must have made the apostles' position very awkward. Had Jesus really revealed himself to Paul and appointed him a leader of equal or even greater status than themselves? Under such circumstances, would it be possible to avoid the implication that Jesus had weighed them in the balance and had found them wanting? Could this have provided an alternative reason why Peter, James and John might have invented the story of the Transfiguration—to counteract the threat that this newcomer represented, and to show that they had always been well aware of who Jesus really was?

There would appear to be little doubt that Paul gradually did take centre stage in the fulfilment of God's purposes as most of the original disciples faded into obscurity, although to be fair, some of them may have been responsible for the spread of the Gospel to the East. If this was the case, because no written records of such activity were produced (or at least no records ever survived), they have never received the accolades that perhaps they deserve.

In contrast to Luke's version, Paul specifically tells us that he did not go to Jerusalem any time soon after his conversion experience. Instead, he "*did not consult any man*" (Galatians 1:16) but immediately went into Arabia, later returning to Damascus. Paul claims that he did not visit Jerusalem until three years after his conversion, and when he did, the only apostle that he met was Peter, although he also mentions seeing James, the Lord's brother. After this he did not go to Jerusalem again for fourteen years (Galatians 2:1).

It is very difficult to square these different accounts with any notion of Luke having been anything other than a fringe member among Paul's travelling companions, irrespective of the "we" passage in Acts 16:9-18, the reference to "us" in Acts 21:18 and even Paul's reference to "*Our dear friend Luke*" (Colossians 4:14). Paul may have known Luke as a fellow Christian brother but the evidence rather points to Luke having a very scanty knowledge of Paul's life and putting together an account of Paul's travels and message that are largely conjecture and based on hearsay.

The account of Paul's defence before the crowd reads as if was taken from a record of the court proceedings for the day, and all fundamentalists and many evangelicals would like to believe that this was the case. However, it merely reaffirms that Luke could not have been present at any of these events and that his account is the result of his need to fill in the gaps to produce a coherent story. It is what all modern writers have to do when they produce dramas about the lives of famous people, and it is what is referred to as "poetic licence". It certainly removes any notion that he was writing factual history under the inspiration of the Holy Spirit.

If this is the case with the Acts of the Apostles, there is no reason to suppose it was any different when he wrote his Gospel. Indeed, if Luke's version of events is questionable, then all the other Gospels must be seen as equally questionable and we are left with little or nothing that we can be certain about, except probably the fact that someone called Jesus existed, that he was a very influential person as a result of both his personality and his message, and that this influence was able to survive his execution by crucifixion.

Did Paul find Peter and the other apostles to be of limited education and possibly limited intelligence and look down on them? Was this, at least in part, at the root of the tension that seems to have existed between them? Perhaps he considered them incapable of comprehending the full significance of the Gospel as he had come to understand it? Whichever way, Paul the outsider was to become by far the most influential of all the followers of Jesus. The truth is that Paul probably had the greatest hand of anybody in formulating the Gospel as we know it today. The Jewish brand of Christianity, put abroad by the original apostles, simply disappeared into the mists of time, possibly wiped out by the Roman armies during the Jewish rebellion of CE 66-70.

Perhaps there is one other issue that needs to be mentioned. Luke's account of Acts ends in the most unsatisfactory manner, leaving the fate of Paul in limbo. This raises an important question. If Paul was still alive when Luke was writing, and Luke was able to visit him, why did Luke not use the opportunity to do so and obtain more details and a more reliable version of Paul's conversion? Is the answer that Paul was, in fact, dead by the time Luke was writing? Was Luke's ultimate purpose to preserve the memory of Paul for posterity, just as he had attempted to do for Jesus with his Gospel account? Was the enormous influence that Paul had had, not only on the development of the early Church but also on the life of Luke himself, the reason that we now have the narrative that we refer to as The Acts of the Apostles?

7   FURTHER ISSUES IN ACTS

Not only does Peter perform the miracle of healing the crippled beggar at the gate of the Temple but we are told that the early Church prayed for such miracles (Acts 4:30) and God granted their request (Acts 5:12). Miracles appeared to occur in abundance. We then find that miracles were not confined to the apostles alone, those who could claim to be "special", but Stephen also performed great wonders and miraculous signs. Among other miracles, both Peter and Paul healed lame people (Acts 3:1-8; 14:7-9), raised people from the dead (Acts 9:36-42; 20:9-12) and experienced miraculous escapes from prison (Acts 12:5-11; 16:25-30). Paul himself claims that his ministry was authenticated by signs and miracles (Romans 15:19; 2 Corinthians 12:12).

This issue of miracles goes back to Luke's conception of the day of Pentecost. On that day the disciples presumably received the "*power from on high*" that Jesus had promised (Luke 24:49; Acts 1:8). Luke is quite clear that this special experience achieved in one moment what Jesus had been unable to achieve during his entire ministry, including the forty days following the Resurrection: understanding. Furthermore, it was not the fact of the Resurrection that changed the disciples into fearless evangelists but rather the experience of being baptised with the Holy Spirit. The disciples appear to have had more than one such experience of being filled with the Spirit (Acts 4:31). On each occasion it was an unmistakable event.

It almost seems to suggest that to become a member of this new movement it was necessary to have a special experience that produced supernatural enlightenment (as well as bestowing special powers) almost making it a gnostic gospel.

If this experience really was the driving force that ignited the early Christian movement, what can be said of today's Church? Even the Pentecostal Church and more lately the charismatic churches, have never approached anything that could be compared to what Luke seems to be describing, despite their fanciful claims. Indeed, having spent many, many hours in Pentecostal gatherings and some charismatic meetings "seeking the Spirit", I have to say that I believe the whole thing is a sham and nothing beyond an exercise in self-delusion. Neither I, nor anybody else to my knowledge, could claim to have experienced what Luke says the disciples experienced, and there is not a single person anywhere in the world who can say, as Peter did, "*What I have, I give you.*"

Paul refers to Luke as a beloved physician or doctor (Colossians 4:14). Doctors would have been herbalists among other things and so Luke may well have been familiar with hallucinogenic drugs. Such drugs are said to produce "out of this world" experiences, and people still seek such experiences in our own day. It is hard to believe that people now are any different from our ancient ancestors. John Allegro of Dead Sea Scrolls fame and author of *The Sacred Mushroom and the Cross*, believed that drugs played a part in many ancient religious cults. Could they ever have played a part in any religious meeting that Luke may have witnessed? This is not to suggest that the early Church indulged in this kind of thing. It is simply to say that we cannot rule out the fact that some church or churches may have strayed into these areas and Luke was aware of one or more that did, or that he was familiar with drug-induced hallucinations in other religious cults and he was influenced by this when he created his account of the experience of the baptism with the Holy Spirit at Pentecost.

There are many reasons offered as to why miracles are no longer evident in the Church today, and there is little hard evidence to suggest their existence despite the obsession with healing ministries and healing crusades. There is one reason, however, that is only infrequently advanced (certainly in Christian circles), and that is that miracles may never have occurred, either in the life of Jesus or in the life of the early Church. Luke, despite the many beautiful features of his Gospel, does appear to have been very gullible and superstitious. The credibility of the narrative in the Acts of the Apostles must be considered as being very low. I would suggest that the miraculous accounts in Acts are almost certainly the product of the superstitious age in which he lived and only retain credibility today because many of us, despite all our modern knowledge, are every bit as gullible as he was.

It is interesting to note that the Venerable Bede (672/3-735 CE), commonly regarded as the father of English history, wrote an account of the history of the English people from the time of Caesar's excursions into England in 55 and 54 BCE until Bede's own time, specifically chronicling the arrival and growth of the Christian Church. Although both this account and many other works of Bede's are highly regarded, he makes reference to many supposed miracles which he appears to accept as a matter of course. These supposed miracles caused him no more problem than the supposed miracles in Acts caused Luke. When religious people write (or talk) about their faith, there appears to be a tendency to uncritical acceptance of the supernatural. The accounts in Acts and Bede's writings share one thing in common—neither author would appear to have been an eyewitness of the miraculous events that they describe. Such events always seem to be more believable when they happened long ago and preferably far away.

To accept the fact that the miraculous events recorded by Luke in Acts probably have little basis in fact has had one significant advantage from my point of view. It has finally stopped me from engaging in what turned out to be a fruitless search for some supernatural experience and a supernatural power that do not exist, and also from having an obsession with miracles because they almost certainly did not happen. I know that I am not alone in having struggled with this issue. The Internet is awash with discussions on this theme, with a huge range of opinion, all emanating from professing Christians. It is one more example of the Holy Spirit failing to guide the people of God into all truth.

8 THE GOSPELS

We now come to the problem of the Gospels themselves and our lack of knowledge regarding them. We do not know when they were first committed to writing, although, as noted earlier, Christian belief had probably developed, possibly considerably, before such writing occurred, and all the accounts were almost certainly predated by Paul's various letters. We cannot be certain who wrote them and we do we know for certain whether any of the Gospel writers were familiar with each other's writings, since copying manuscripts for distribution must have been a difficult and slow process. It does seem rather unlikely, however, that anyone who knew of the existence of one complete Gospel account would then chose to write a full, rival account of his own.

Luke probably wrote his Gospel as a necessary prelude to his story of the early Church, further suggesting that he was not aware of the existence any other major account of Jesus's life. If he was aware of other accounts, it is very difficult to explain why his narrative differs in crucial ways from the other Gospel accounts, particularly his assertion that the disciples were instructed to remain in Jerusalem after the Resurrection. We do not know if any of them used other material, earlier writings that were not preserved, perhaps because the need to do so disappeared as fuller versions of the Gospel were produced.

Writing is a skill that needs to be learned and would not have been widespread in those days but would have been the preserve of an educated elite of specialist scribes. It is by no means impossible that writers who wished to impart more gravitas to what they were writing, particularly if the subject was deemed to be of immense importance, would write under an assumed identity, an identity that would lend the necessary aura of authority to what they were communicating. We cannot automatically assume when a writer implies that he is a disciple or even the "*the disciple whom Jesus loved*" (John 21:20) and claims to be the "*disciple who testifies to these things and who wrote them down*" (John 21:24) that we are actually reading an eyewitness account of events.

The idea of producing written accounts of Jesus's life is unlikely to have been of immediate concern for the early believers and it is possible that no attempt was made before belief in an early return of Jesus crystallised, at which point the need would have no longer have existed. The need would have arisen only as time went by, Jesus had not returned, and the major players aged or died or some other cataclysmic event affecting all regions threatened the entire existence of the movement. The beliefs of the movement by this time could, and probably would have undergone considerable development, because that is in the nature of orally transmitted knowledge or beliefs. Things do not become set in concrete until they have been written down. That is one of the great powers of the written word—the words themselves are no longer subject to change.

Before the written accounts, stories about Jesus could have continued to grow, new interpretations being imposed on many of the remembered events of his life. Eventually there would be plenty of such new interpretations and no doubt different stories occurred in different regions. Separating fact from fiction would have become an impossible task. All that we can claim to possess is a snapshot of the beliefs about Jesus that existed at the time that the accounts of his life were written down. Once written and sufficiently copied, however, they would have served to exert a unifying influence and limit further variations of belief. The lack of any certain knowledge regarding the dates of authorship is unfortunate. It does place a limit on what we can ever expect to know about beliefs that the Church claims will determine our eternal destiny.

The belief that the Gospels represent any kind of accurate, factual account of the life of Jesus, therefore, is almost certainly misplaced. Jesus does not seem to have been understood by his close disciples during his lifetime. The understanding that he was the "only begotten Son of God" must have developed later, even if we allow for only a relatively short time after the crucifixion.

However, once this belief had developed, it would have been impossible for people to turn back the clock to the period of his lifetime. Everything would now be seen through the eyes of faith. The Gospels we have almost certainly reflect the Jesus of faith and not any historically accurate portrait of his life. This, of course, presents us with a huge problem. Jesus, understood as the "Son of God", would have to be a very different person from Jesus, the carpenter's son from Nazareth, or even Jesus the charismatic Jewish rabbi. He would have to be greater than any of the Old Testament prophets. They would have to ascribe to him supernatural powers. This new concept of Jesus must have become standard belief at an early stage, possibly before Paul came on the scene.

Hence, the Jesus presented in the Gospels is not a Jesus who could have been overtaken by the events surrounding the crucifixion. He had to be a Jesus who was always in control, someone who eclipsed all who had gone before him. Did Moses cause the Red (Reed) Sea to part? Jesus would walk upon the water. Did Moses bring forth water from the rock to quench the thirst of the Israelites? Jesus would turn water into wine to satisfy the thirst of the guests at a wedding feast. Were the children of Israel miraculously fed with manna in the wilderness during Moses' time and did Elisha multiply the oil to help a needy prophet's widow? Jesus would feed the multitudes with a few loaves and fishes on two occasions. Did Elijah control the elements on Mount Carmel? Jesus would control the wind and waves and calm the storm on Lake Galilee. Did Elisha cure Naaman, a foreign army commander, of leprosy? Jesus would also heal the lepers. Did Elisha restore the Shunammite woman's son to life? Jesus would also raise the dead. A new Jesus would have to be created, based upon the real Jesus but now with a mythical element. This Jesus was to be the miracle-working Son of God, who assumed all the attributes of God when he forgave sins and calmed the storm (see Psalm 65:7); a Jesus who prophesied his own death and his own resurrection, who said "*No-one takes it* [his life] *from me, but I lay it down of my own accord. I have authority to lay it down and authority to take it up again*" (John 10:18). Just how much the Gospels might have been mythologized is impossible to say, but any mythologizing at all causes immense uncertainty for us today.

That the understanding of Jesus's life underwent considerable development is evidenced by the Gospel of St. John, probably the last Gospel to be written and radically different from the other three Gospels. It focuses on the person of Jesus from beginning to end. Not here the occasional allusion to the real purpose of Jesus's life. Little time is given over to moral issues (the lovely story of the woman taken in adultery in John 8:1-11 appears to have been a later addition). No parables illustrating moral truths or describing the kingdom are included.

Instead we have eight great "I am" statements of Jesus. "*Before Abraham was born, I am!*" he proclaims (John 8:58). He is the bread of life, the light of the world, the door, the good shepherd, the resurrection and the life, the way, the truth and the life and finally the true vine. Here is recorded the great miracle of the raising of Lazarus, as if the scale of the miracles was exaggerated with every new account. And it is in this Gospel that Jesus receives the highest accolade when "doubting" Thomas addresses him as "*My Lord and my God!*" (John 20:28). In this Gospel, the world is divided into two groups on one simple criterion: those who believed that Jesus was the Christ or Messiah and those who rejected that claim.

This exaltation of Jesus reaches its apogee in the last book of the Bible, Revelation, which is also imputed to the disciple John. In chapter 22, a chapter incidentally that begins with a glorious vision of life in the eternal city, one which totally eclipses all previous conceptions of any kingdom, we find Jesus making the following statements: "*I am the Alpha and the Omega, the First and Last, the Beginning and the End*" (v 13). In Revelation 1:8, The Lord God is the Alpha and the Omega. Then: "*I am the Root and the Offspring of David, and the bright Morning Star*" (v 16). The last phrase appears to be a reference to Venus, which occupied a place of considerable significance in a number of ancient pagan religious cults. Finally, in verse 20, we read: "*He who testifies to these things says, 'Yes I am coming* **soon**. *Amen. Come, Lord Jesus'*" [emphasis added]. We are, of course, still waiting.

The Jesus presented in the Gospels is not a Jesus who would have been acceptable to traditional Jews and this suggests that the Gospels were probably written after the fall of Jerusalem (70 CE) when many Jews would have had to consider a reinterpretation of their faith and there would have been little reason left to consider traditional Jewish sensibilities. It is very difficult to imagine such accounts being in circulation in Jerusalem before that time, particularly as there was a Jewish Church in the city that seemed to coexist side by side with traditional Judaism. They could, possibly, have been written in predominantly Gentile areas at an earlier date, but they do suggest a post-70 CE understanding of their world. The writers bend over backwards to exculpate the Romans from any blame for the crucifixion, but seemingly no longer care about offending the Jews. Even the most Jewish of the Gospel writers, Matthew, has the Jews cry out "*Let his blood be on us and on our children*" (Matthew 27:25). Is this

Matthew's way of accounting for the magnitude of the disaster that had overtaken his fellow citizens—they were being punished for their rejection of Jesus?

Today, we have the same problem that the Gospel writers had. Most people who read the Bible will have been conditioned to believe that Jesus was the Son of God. In such a situation, miracles do not present a problem. Once you possess that mind-set, it is impossible to view Jesus as a human being with any limitations that were not self-imposed. If the Gospel writers were not writing actual fact, then nobody at the time would have known, and even when they did have to invent details, they would simply incorporate into the narrative the common beliefs of their age with never a thought that they might be straying into fantasy.

Any hopes that we might have of discovering actual truth are non-existent because there are no tests that we can apply in this instance to verify the truth. Religious literature and historical literature are totally different genres. The first century and the twenty-first century are just as different and we cannot appreciate their world any more than they would appreciate ours. To accord to the first century Christians more faith, more spiritual receptiveness, more spiritual understanding and more integrity than we have today is neither helpful nor very likely to have been the case. It will not bring us any closer to understanding the Jesus of whom the authors of the Gospels wrote. We only know that he was a figure of immense and lasting influence and we can only be grateful that they left us any record of what he taught and the kind of person he may have been. The glimpse they give us is, in many ways, one of unsurpassed beauty.

9   THE BEATITUDES AND OTHER ISSUES

When we come to look at the teachings of Jesus, both Matthew and Luke contain sayings that are described as beatitudes. The only problem is that two of the beatitudes contained in these Gospels have totally different meanings. In Matthew 5:3 and 5:6, we read *"Blessed are the poor **in spirit"** and "Blessed are those who hunger and thirst **for righteousness"*** [emphasis added]. In Luke 6:20-21, however, it reads simply: *"Blessed are you who are poor"* and *"Blessed are you who hunger now."*

Luke makes it absolutely clear that he is referring to lack of material things and physical hunger, because he goes on to say, in verses 24 and 25: *"But woe to you who are rich, for you have already received your comfort"* and *"Woe to you who are well fed now, for you will go hungry."* That would make no sense if these statements were referring to spiritual matters. Why should people who were spiritually rich have those riches taken from them? Also, Luke seems to emphasise his point with the story of the rich man and a poor man named Lazarus (Luke 16:19-31). He is the only one to record this parable. Lazarus seems to be accepted in heaven solely because he was poor in the material sense while he was on earth. The rich man was condemned for failing to share his good fortune with his less fortunate neighbour.

Luke's version of these two beatitudes raises huge problems. I have lived in two countries (other than England), both of which had extreme poverty among significant sections of the population. Poverty is hardly a blessing. Poor people suffer poorer health, poorer education, fewer opportunities or choices and shorter life spans. I remember David Shepherd, when he was the Bishop of Liverpool, drawing attention to exactly the same issue in our own society in the 1980s and there is no reason to believe that much the same situation does not exist today. My mother's oft recounted stories of the grinding poverty that she experienced when growing up, and the resentment that it produced in her, are still indelibly etched on my mind.

There is a thread in the Gospels that suggests that once God has provided us with the things essential to daily living, we should not seek anything beyond that. Such ideas are a far cry from the Prosperity Gospel where you can have your cake and eat it, where the abundance of God's provision is not confined solely to the realms of paradise but is available in the here and now.

I have always experienced a tension between Luke's seeming exaltation of poverty and the natural desire that I have, and probably all others have, to better ourselves and, in particular, to try and ensure that our children have a better life than we have had. The desire to build on the achievements of previous generations seems to me to be inherent in human nature and provides the stimulus for progress; it is what distinguishes us from the rest of creation and it is essential to what we are. Surely this cannot be a bad thing? Who wants to remain static and reinvent the wheel every day? That sort of existence would condemn us to be little better than the animals, not give us the exalted status accorded to us in the Bible of being just a little lower than the angels (Hebrews 2:7).

In mediaeval Europe, the practice of usury, the lending of money at interest, was condemned by the Church. In the Old Testament, Jews were forbidden to lend money at interest to fellow Jews, but could do so to non-Jews (Deuteronomy 23:20). According to Naill Ferguson, in his book *The Ascent of Money,* it was precisely these facts that led the Jews to dominate the emerging banking systems in renaissance Europe (page 35). The love of money is certainly condemned in the New Testament (1 Timothy 6:10). However, history seems to suggest that if some people had not had a love for money, modern financial institutions may never have developed and progress would have been greatly impeded.

Though we may not like to admit it, people's love of money drives capitalism and capitalism has raised the standard of living, not just for the few, but for many, many people and beyond all expectations. Capitalism is a system with many flaws, its failure to control rampant greed being among them. It does cause inequality and envy. However, it is certainly a far superior system to anything that Jesus knew of, and no-one to date has conclusively shown that there is a better alternative. Capitalism does generate wealth and the overall benefits to society do seem to be greater in countries that have a broadly capitalist economic system than in countries that have tried other options, the recent banking problems notwithstanding.

I, and many others, have been able to become home owners precisely because of the sophisticated financial institutions of the country that we live in. I have relatives in Peru who have had considerably more difficulty in becoming home owners because Peru does not have any mortgage facilities. Potential entrepreneurs find it (or possibly used to find it) equally difficult to borrow money to set up in business. People who have lived in developing countries are often acutely aware of the difficulties that this can entail. Being a home owner offers me security and provides me with collateral should I need to borrow money from a bank; it gives me some sort of stake in society and probably contributes to my being a more responsible person. In other words, we have benefited, as a society, from a lot of the good that has come from some people having had a love for money and a proper appreciation of how this love can to put to good use.

Luke's version of the teaching of Jesus would, presumably, have resulted in a world where material progress may never have occurred. Most evangelical Christians of today ignore Luke's interpretation in favour of the Prosperity Gospel. Some of America's best known Christians are also exceedingly wealthy and in many cases they have, directly or indirectly, made their money as a result of activities connected to their faith, particularly from writing books or being involved in television ministry.

In one rendering of the non-canonical Gospel of Thomas (The Scholars Translation by Stephen Patterson and Marvin Mayer, available on the Internet), the second half of verse 69 says: "*Congratulations to those who go hungry, so the stomach of the one in want may be filled.*" This is a third version of this beatitude, different from the two mentioned previously, but one that makes perfect sense, and one that is certainly consistent with the image of Jesus that I have. The very fact that such writings exist indicates the enormous difficulty in knowing exactly what Jesus taught, and probably reflects the vagaries of memory and the differences of understanding that were the reality when the Gospel accounts were written.

The Gospel of Thomas may not have been available as a complete Gospel in written form when the canon of Scripture was fixed, although there are references to parts of it by some of the early Church Fathers. However, it could never have been included in any canon of Scripture because it presents an entirely different message, one in which salvation is gained through knowledge and understanding, not through the death of Jesus and the forgiveness of sins. There are no details of Jesus's life, and no mention of his death or resurrection. It is simply concerned with what Jesus is supposed to have taught. In the opening sentence it claims that: "*These are the secret sayings that the living Jesus spoke and Didymos Judas Thomas recorded.*" In John 20:24, "Doubting Thomas" is also called Didymus (a slight spelling difference). There are some very strange, unintelligible sayings in this Gospel, but nearly half of it contains teaching that is recognisable in the four canonical Gospels. A complete version of the Gospel of Thomas was not discovered (in Egypt) until 1945, but the manuscript is ancient and we cannot discount the possibility that, in its day, it may have been the only written document available to some believers.

The Gospel of Thomas also furnishes us with an interesting picture of the status of women around that time. The very last verse of the document (which apparently was added at some later date) reads: "Simon Peter said to them, '*Make Mary [Magdalene] leave us, for females don't deserve life.*'" Jesus said *"Look, I will guide her to make her male, so that she too may become a living spirit resembling you males. For every female who makes herself male will enter the kingdom of heaven.*" It is interesting to note that, even by the day of Pentecost, the Bible has ceased to mention any of the women who figured in the Gospel narratives. They are consigned to oblivion, a fact that may indicate a deliberate policy of excluding women from any positions of influence.

There are other worrying examples of sayings of Jesus which seem to contradict our modern understanding of him. In Matthew 5:17-19, Jesus seems to be an ultra-orthodox Jew, insisting on the unchangeable foundation of the (Mosaic) Law. In Mark 10:5 however, Jesus seems to challenge what Moses decreed about divorce. Does this passage in Matthew represent the real Jesus or does it just reflect Matthew's passionate allegiance to all things Jewish?

In Matthew 8:5-13, there is a story about Jesus healing a centurion's servant. In this account, Jesus is in Capernaum and the centurion himself went to Jesus with his request. In Luke's account of the same story (Luke 7:1-10), the centurion asks some of the Jewish elders to go to Jesus on his behalf and ask for the favour. In John 4:46-53, there is what I can only assume is another account of the same story, although this time, Jesus is in the Galilean town, or more probably village, of Cana. John mentions two visits that Jesus made to Cana and also tells us that Nathanael, one of the twelve disciples, hailed from

Cana, but it is not mentioned in any other Gospel and its location is unknown.

This time, in John's account, the approach is again made in person, not by a Roman centurion but by a certain royal official, presumably an official at the court of King Herod, and the sick person is not his servant but his son. The son, however, does lie ill in Capernaum, not Cana. Both Matthew and John make reference to the time at which the servant/son recovered, and in each case it was the exact time that Jesus made his reply. There is enough overlap in all these stories to accept that they all refer to the same event, but not enough agreement to suggest that the Holy Spirit was inspiring any of the writers or "guiding them into all truth" (John 16:13), or that the Bible is a factually accurate document, much less an inerrant one.

This story, which appears to be set in different locations, is, perhaps, reminiscent of a more modern story that I heard Dr Alan Redpath once tell, the details of which are mentioned in my previous book, *Our Gay Son*.

10 THE PROMISES AND LEGACY OF JESUS

It may never be possible to resolve problems regarding the historicity and accuracy of the Gospel accounts. We can, however, look at promises that Jesus makes towards the end of his life and also one very important prayer, all of which occur in John's Gospel, and which permit an element of what we might call critical or even scientific scrutiny. In John 14:12, Jesus says: "*I tell you the truth, anyone who has faith in me will do what I have been doing. He will do even greater things than these because I am going to the Father.*" That is a promise that needs hardly any discussion. Its fulfilment has not occurred, certainly if Jesus performed all the miracles attributed to him in the Gospels. However, this has not prevented many fanciful explanations being offered to explain its supposed fulfilment.

In the same chapter and in chapter 16, Jesus repeats a promise three times over. The promise, essentially, is that Jesus "*will ask the Father and he will give you another Counsellor to be with you for ever—the Spirit of truth" (v 16 & 17) and "the Holy Spirit, whom the Father will send in my name will teach you all things*" (v 26) and will guide them into all truth (16:13). There is no evidence that the Holy Spirit was intended for the immediate disciples of Jesus only, and the Church throughout the ages has always believed itself to be guided by the Holy Spirit. In John 17:20, Jesus prays specifically, not just for the disciples alone, but for "*all those who will believe in me through their message"* and his prayer is that *"they may be brought to complete unity"* (v 23). How far have either the promises been fulfilled or this prayer been answered? The two are not of course entirely separate issues. If we are not led into all truth, there is little hope that we can have any unity. And we do not need to look very far to see that there is little unity, suggesting that we have not been led into all truth.

For all the pious platitudes about underlying unity that we might hear from Church leaders today, all the evidence points the other way. There is no single understanding of the Christian Gospel. When the Roman Emperor Constantine made Christianity an accepted religion of the Empire (313 CE) and seemingly embraced it as his own preferred religion, he seemed to become concerned by the lack of clearly defined doctrine. He eventually called together the recognised Bishops of the day to formulate an "official" version of the faith, and they met in Nicaea in 325 CE for this purpose. The doctrine of the Trinity was first established here, but it represented a majority view, not a unanimous one. Important Bishops on the losing side (notably Arius) were sent into exile.

Further Councils occurred in 381, 449 and 451 because "heresy" did not die away. There have been many other Councils and from these various Creeds have emerged and also been modified. The three important Creeds are the Apostles' Creed, the Nicene Creed and the Athanasius Creed. They are similar but have technical differences. All creeds are an attempt to impose a rigid set of beliefs on adherents of the faith. They have aroused fierce passions and caused much bloodshed. But who is to say where ultimate truth lies? Who can be sure that the Apostles' Creed, as it is today, is the result of the inspiration of the Holy Spirit? Is the majority opinion always the correct one?

The problem with forming rigid creeds is what to do with those who fail to adhere to such creeds, or those who have a different viewpoint. Who decides when someone is a heretic or is guilty of blasphemy? It was to prove an inevitable slippery slope leading ultimately to the office of the Inquisition, the inhuman instrument used by the Roman Catholic Church over hundreds of years for enforcing conformity. The Inquisitors, special envoys of the Pope, were, without question, among the vilest people who have ever involved themselves with religion. How many suffered appalling tortures at the hands of these men for no greater a crime than that of being presumed to have views or beliefs that were even slightly different from those approved by the Church? Indeed, how much wealth did the Vatican acquire by confiscating the land and property of monasteries whose occupants were conveniently deemed to hold heretical beliefs? Jesus may not have wanted such a thing, and almost certainly never envisaged such a thing. It was just an unintended consequence that resulted from the formation of the organisation that his life gave birth to.

In 1517, a Roman Catholic monk named Martin Luther challenged several practices within the Church of his day. He precipitated the Reformation which, over time, resulted in the formation of various Protestant churches, including, indirectly, the Anglican Church in England. Reformation Theology gave rise to differences of belief that were by no means trivial. For the next three hundred years or so Catholics and Protestants intermittently slaughtered each other on account of these differences. Northern Ireland is testimony to the enduring bitterness between the two factions. Not much unity to be seen here. Evangelical Christians, for the most part, do not see Roman Catholics or liberal Protestants as being true Christians at all.

The USA is one of the most religious nations on planet Earth. Yet there are hundreds of different denominations and many totally independent Churches, probably all of the latter having fundamentalist beliefs. Many of these different groups believe that they alone possess the whole truth. Christian has fought Christian over the issues of slavery, segregation, and now homosexuality. There is little agreement on issues such as abortion, women priests, the Baptism in the Holy Spirit, speaking in tongues and a host of other matters.

Again, some Christians point to an underlying unity of belief, with disagreements being over non-essentials. Jesus, however, promised that the Holy Spirit would lead his followers into *all* truth, not just essential truth. He prayed for unity among his followers. History shows that human beings are not capable of agreeing or agreeing to differ. Toleration does not figure very highly on the list of human virtues. Jesus's prayer was a non-starter. One only has to look at the last Lambeth Conference to know this. The kind of surface unity that these types of conference produce is a million miles away from anything that Jesus could have had in mind.

Religion is not all good. Some of it is, probably a lot of it is, but certainly not all of it. It is a mixture of the good, the not-so-good and, occasionally, the downright ugly. And the reason is that religion, by its very nature, produces disagreement and division. If we disagree, and I am right, then you must be wrong. Religion also affects the emotions. Strongly held beliefs produce passion and passion combined with opposing viewpoints makes for an explosive mixture.

The inescapable truth is that the promises of Jesus have not been fulfilled and the prayers of Jesus do not seem to have been answered. Jesus appears to have been hugely optimistic about God's willingness to answer prayer. "*Ask and it will be given to you*" he says (see Matt 7:7-12; Luke 11:9-13). In the parable of the persistent widow (Luke 18:1-8) he suggests that determined prayer will bring quick and definite answers. He promises that if we "*seek first his* [God's] *kingdom and his righteousness all these* [other necessary] *things will be given to you as well*" (Matt 6:33).

Thousands of Christians have prayed for the people of Zimbabwe but Christians and non-Christians alike who happen to live there seem to have suffered equally if they have been outside of President Mugabe's largesse. Has God speedily answered prayers to remove Mugabe from power? Have not Christians and non-Christians suffered equally from circumstances beyond their control throughout history? The optimism of Jesus does not seem to have been particularly well-founded. It raises serious questions that go to the very heart of faith.

There is one further issue that we need to confront. There is an underlying assumption, certainly among Christians, that Christianity was the major force that brought civilisation to Western Europe. However, there is a lot of truth in the belief that the rise of Christianity to the status of official religion of the Roman Empire in 380 CE was detrimental to the progress of civilisation. Christianity suffered from one major drawback. It seemed to look askance on all knowledge that did not pertain to religious faith and showed no interest in preserving the knowledge acquired over centuries by other cultures, notably that of the Greeks.

It seems very possible that a Christian rabble, at the instigation of Bishop Cyril, was involved in a major destruction of the library at Alexandria early in the fifth century, a crime that must rank as one of the greatest of all crimes against civilisation, although this may not have been the only time that the library was attacked. At the same time, the Greek woman philosopher and mathematician, Hypatia, was savagely murdered on the streets by the same rabble. As the Church grew in strength, the West descended into a period of intellectual stagnation which lasted roughly from the fall of Rome in 476 to the fourteenth century and the Renaissance period. This was a time in which the Church vied with kings and emperors for political power, and could stand accused of being a major contributor to the stagnation but certainly not of helping to lead the European world out of it.

In fact, since the birth of the modern scientific era about 400 years ago, the Christian Church has persistently opposed major advances in scientific understanding when such advances have in any way been perceived to be in opposition to Bible teaching. Its current opposition to modern views of homosexuality therefore stands in a long tradition of opposition to any enlightenment that appears to be of human origin. Any nation that majors in religious knowledge to the neglect of other kinds of knowledge is a nation destined for stagnation and trouble. Unfortunately, Jesus himself gives the impression of believing that knowledge of God is the only knowledge really worth having. The Church that is his legacy has often seemed to believe exactly the same thing. Only the massive and undeniable benefits of modern science appear to have succeeded in persuading a reluctant Church to adopt a more enlightened view.

11   THE LIFE AND MESSAGE OF JESUS

What can we say with reasonable certainty, or even reasonable likelihood, about the life of Jesus? The answer to that question is probably very little. The Bible tells us that he grew in wisdom (Luke 2:52). Thus the knowledge that he had must have been acquired in the same way that everybody else acquired knowledge, by receiving what was passed down in his culture. As a Jew from a typical Jewish village, his formal education would have consisted of little, if anything, beyond rote learning of the Jewish Scriptures and learning to appreciate Jewish history and Jewish beliefs. Beyond this there were simple trades to be learned and practical matters of farming to be mastered.

However, he must have been exposed to all the superstitious beliefs of his day and he certainly seems to have accepted the belief in demons and the fact that demonic possession was responsible for many illnesses and even physical disabilities. In other words, his knowledge and experience would have been limited to the very narrow confines of the world in which he lived, even if we allow for a supernatural understanding of the Scriptures that he learned.

In the early part of 2011 I watched a programme on Channel 4 about Islamic education in Northern Nigeria. The "education" consisted of learning the Qur'ân by rote, in Arabic. Parents seemed desperate for their sons to be given this opportunity. The regime in the school was harsh and boys were sent to beg on the streets, each being given a quota, before afternoon lessons. This was necessary to ensure food for both students and teachers, although one can imagine that the teachers might have done rather well out of all this, by the standards of the society in which they lived. It is not clear what end result the parents of the boys hoped for, except that in some way they seemed to feel it a duty to make sure that their sons where instructed in the Muslim faith. What is certain is that after all this brainwashing they would not be fitted for living life in a modern society. Western viewers watching this sort of thing are likely to be appalled by such ignorance and angry that young lives should be wasted in this manner. However, this is something that is not simply confined to backward cultures.

Around the time that I want to Africa, an Asian Muslim family came to live next door but one to my mother. They were extremely pleasant and though the parents were very religious, it seemed that the younger members of the family were quite westernised and viewed the religion of their parents with mild toleration, even expecting that it might die away along with the older generation. I also got to know them quite well at a later date. They were, indeed, a very pleasant, friendly, generous, hard-working and ambitious family.

One of the boys, a third generation member of the family, was very bright and eventually went to university to study dentistry. However, the family's pride in this achievement was overshadowed by their pride in the fact that he could recite over three quarters of the Qur'ân in Arabic. Perhaps by now he can recite all of it. My own mind boggles at such a feat. I am not even sure that he understands any of the Arabic that he can recite. Yet, so strong is the Islamic religion in this family now that this useless brainwashing is viewed as a great pinnacle of achievement. It is just fortunate that his education has been supplemented by something else a little more useful. The boys in Nigeria were not so lucky.

Bizarre as this kind of thing may appear to us, we need to confront the fact that the education that Jesus received was no doubt very similar to that received by these African boys. It was not designed to enable Jesus to take his place in an increasingly Hellenised world. It was designed to preserve Jewish culture and a Jewish way of life that was totally dominated by their religion, and in this respect it had much in common with many Islamic communities in various parts of the world today.

Jesus seems to have absorbed his people's scriptures with considerable enthusiasm and his fascination with them is revealed in an incident, recorded only by Luke (Luke 2:41-52), where, as a twelve year old, he gets left behind in Jerusalem and is found some days later among the teachers of the law in the temple courts. His knowledge and understanding of the scriptures is said to have astonished these experts. It seems very unlikely however, that Jesus would have had much exposure to the Hellenistic (Greek) culture and ideas of the age.

We have no evidence that Jesus was able to speak Greek. Revealingly, the four Gospels contain no reference to any visit of Jesus either to the city of Sepphoris, about 5 km (just over 3 miles) to the north-west of Nazareth, or to its sister city, Tiberias, on the western shore of Lake Galilee. Herod Antipas, one of the sons of Herod the Great, had enlarged, modernised and fortified the city of Sepphoris after it had suffered considerable damage following a Jewish revolt against Rome around the time that Jesus would have been born. It was the principal city in the province of Galilee for many years, until displaced by Tiberias, and was a centre for trade and for Roman administration, well-connected to other major cities by Roman roads. Within a one hour walking distance from Nazareth, both Joseph and Jesus may have found work there during the rebuilding programme. Jesus must have visited the city many times and, as he was likely to have attracted attention on account of his obvious ability, he could have studied there at some Jewish centre.

Herod built Tiberias from scratch on an old site, naming it in honour of the Roman emperor of the time. Both of these cities, probably built so as not to give overt offence to the Jews, nevertheless had significant Gentile populations and Hellenistic values. Tiberias is less than twenty miles from Nazareth and less than ten miles from Capernaum. In fact, it was probably just an easy boat trip from Capernaum to Tiberias, along the western shore of the lake.

There is no mention, either, of any visit by Jesus to the great city of Caesarea, the port city built by Herod the Great on the eastern shore of the Mediterranean, in admiration of all things Roman and to further the glory of the emperor. Jesus does seem to have confined his interest mainly to the Jewish town of Capernaum and the Jewish villages dotted throughout the province of Galilee, with only occasional excursions into other regions, particularly to the southern province of Judea, and to Jerusalem. It is, of course, quite possible that

Jesus would not have wished to risk the wrath of Herod, or of the officials that would be permanently stationed in these Herodian cities. Maybe his message of the kingdom did have political overtones that would have rendered visits to these places far too dangerous. Galilee, after all, had a reputation as a highly volatile region for political intrigue and insurrection.

It is difficult to avoid the impression, however, that Jesus was a Jewish rabbi who saw his work as a mission to his own people. He was not one to turn away Gentiles who sought his help, but he certainly does not seem to have made any effort to seek them out. And, more worryingly, when he sends out his twelve disciples to preach the gospel, Matthew tells us that he explicitly instructs them: "*Do not go among the Gentiles or enter any town of the Samaritans*" (Matthew 10:5). Luke's version of the same incident omits this restriction (Luke 9:1-6). This is another indication that Matthew's concerns were almost entirely with the Jewish people. The close disciples of Jesus were all Jewish and appeared to view their message as one intended for Jews even after Jesus's death and resurrection.

The only contact that Jesus chose to make with the Gentile world appears to have been a brief excursion to the region of the Phoenician cities of Tyre and Sidon, now situated in modern Lebanon some thirty to forty miles north-west of Galilee, where he heals the demon-possessed daughter of a Syro-Phoenician woman (Mark 7:24-30). This visit may have been occasioned by a desire to escape the attentions of the Jews for a while because of growing opposition to his ministry.

Clearly, however, Jesus was a sincere and highly intelligent person, possessing great charisma and intense religious convictions. He possessed all the attributes of a born leader: a strong personality coupled with great personal magnetism and a deep understanding of the people to whom he spoke because he was one of them and could empathise with their situation and their concerns. His close disciples were clearly in awe of him, of his confidence, of his seeming power over some sicknesses, of his ability to pray and commune with God. Yet they rarely understood him. On the one hand he was a master story-teller while on the other hand considerable difficulty is involved when trying to unravel his message.

At the beginning of Jesus's ministry, we are told that he went into Galilee proclaiming the good news of God: "*The time has come. The kingdom of God is near, repent and believe the good news [Gospel]*" (Mark 1:14-15). Matthew has a briefer but similar statement (Matthew 4:17). It was not a novel message. John the Baptist was already preaching exactly the same thing before Jesus began his own ministry.

I had often wondered, exactly what was this Gospel, or good news, that Jesus referred to? If you were to ask an evangelical Christian today what was meant by the Gospel, you would be told something along the following lines: *God loves you and he sent his son Jesus to die for your sins. He also raised him from the dead. If you believe this, repent of your sins and invite Jesus to come into your life, and if you confess him to be your Saviour and Lord, you will be saved* (i.e. your name will be written in heaven, your eternal salvation will be guaranteed). Some evangelicals would also include water baptism as an essential requirement and all would expect new believers to undergo (or in the case of some churches, to have undergone as infants) water baptism in order to become full members of the fellowship. The issue of the validity of infant baptism is still a contentious matter among evangelicals, one more cause for lack of unity. The answer that a Roman Catholic Christian would give to the same question might be very different.

In Biblical times, the question was asked in a different way: "*What must I do to be saved*?" It is the answer to that question that constitutes an evangelical understanding of the gospel. The Bible never offers an answer as comprehensive as the one on the opposite page, but gives different answers in different places. It should be realised, however, that brief Bible statements always assume a prior knowledge that would amplify the meaning of any statement. "*Believe on the Lord Jesus Christ,*" for instance, would assume that you had sufficient knowledge about Jesus to know what it was you were being asked to believe. The evangelical answer to the question outlined above is a synthesis that tries to encompass all the essentials of the various Bible answers. It is, of course, simply the starting point. A convert embarks on a journey and is expected to grow in the faith through regular instruction.

No modern version of the Gospel is likely to be what Jesus was talking about at the start of his ministry. Only the Gospel of John remotely gives the impression that this could have been the case (John 3:1-21). The other Gospel writers suggest that it had more to do with the establishment of a new community, a kingdom community that people entered voluntarily and accepted the precepts of this kingdom as Jesus propounded them. Particularly welcome in this community were repentant sinners, the poor and the outcasts of society. Whatever form it was supposed to take, if it was to have any outward manifestation, it is unlikely that it would have had much in common with the visible Church that we see today, often ostentatious and immersed in pomp and ceremony, and, in the case of the Anglican Church in England, specialising in great state occasions.

The whole idea of this kingdom, however, may have a greater significance than we tend to give to it. We have already noted that, as Luke closes one era (the time that Jesus was on earth) and initiates another (the development of the fledgling Church), the disciples still had the expectation that Jesus (or God) was going to establish an independent Jewish state and Jesus does not dismiss this idea. Could this "kingdom vision" have formed a significant part of the Jesus message? Did he convey a vision both of a God and of a "kingdom of God" that excited his audience and elicited an enthusiastic response?

Although it is never quite clear what this kingdom was, it certainly appears to have been something for the here and now. The Lord's Prayer highlights this as Jesus tells his followers to pray that God's will "*be done on earth as it is in heaven*" (Matthew 6:10). Jesus seems to want heaven brought down to the earth. The kingdom may have been envisioned as a community within a community, a community of like-minded people in tune with a God who was not some remote entity, but was like a father concerned for the welfare of his children, someone who knew exactly what they needed

(Matt 6:32) and was more than willing to supply all of these needs if only they would ask him and trust him (Matt 7:7-12). It was unlikely that his vision included any kind of formal, organised entity with structure and a hierarchy, because he seems to have rejected the idea of a political kingdom according to the accounts of his temptations.

There can be little doubt that, in whatever way this kingdom was presented, it constituted a very attractive vision. Jesus refers to finding it being like finding buried treasure or a pearl of great price (Matthew 13:44-46). It would, without question, have been a particularly attractive idea to the poor as he gave them hope by placing special emphasis on the novel idea of God's love for sinners and those on the margins of society. He made no secret of the joy that occurred in heaven when a sinner repented (Luke 15:7) and declared that a main purpose of his mission was "*to seek and to save what was lost.*" (Luke 19:10).

Is it possible that Jesus began his preaching ministry with this captivating vision of a new kingdom at the very heart of his message? It would certainly explain the fact that he seemed to be very popular when he first began, particularly among the ordinary people. We are told that a large crowd "*listened to him with delight*" (Mark 12:37). Could this initial success have influenced him to believe that he had a special place in the purposes of God; that he had been chosen to bring this message of deliverance and hope to the people? Could the idea have been reinforced by some demon-possessed (mentally deranged?) people who referred to him as the Son of God (Mark 1:24 & 5:7)?

It is not clear whether Jesus expected opposition to his preaching, though opposition was fairly predictable. Jesus's message was different. People and their needs were at its heart. This was not the case with most of the religion of Jesus's day, particularly not of those fundamentalist religious fanatics, the Pharisees. In their world, people took a back seat while satisfying the requirements of God took centre-stage. Thus they loaded heavy burdens on people's backs (Luke 11:46) and conjured up endless requirements that no-one could hope to comply with. They delighted in the detail and in crushing people with guilt, leaving them with a sense of hopeless unworthiness. As Jesus astutely observed, they showed rather less enthusiasm for shouldering any such burdens themselves. It was a complete clash of religious ideologies and there was never likely to be any amicable co-existence. Indeed, Jesus went out of his way to contrast what he was talking about with what the Pharisees represented.

A significant turning point, however, may have come when he visited his home town of Nazareth. It was here that he put forward claims to have been anointed to bring the good news to them (Luke 4:18-19). Such claims divide people onto two camps. There are those who seek leadership and respond gladly to someone who, convinced of his own qualifications, offers it. There are others who instinctively resent anyone else who lays claim to be different and in any way superior to others. This latter group consists of ordinary people as well as those who may have climbed the ladder themselves and now resent jumped-up competitors. Perhaps this occasion was the first time that Jesus made special claims for himself and first encountered the resentment of ordinary people as a result. John also tells us that a crisis of this kind occurred at some stage during Jesus's ministry (John 6:60).

Did Jesus begin to shift the focus of his message at this point? We find warnings that any man wishing to follow him must be prepared to "*take up his cross*" (Luke 9:23) and that followers could expect to be "*flogged in the synagogues*" (Matt 10:17). To attract followers under these conditions, emphasis would have had to be laid on rewards in the afterlife. So, we find advice to "*lay up for yourselves treasures in heaven*" (Matt 6:20) and the promise that "*great is your reward in heaven*" (Matt 5:12; Luke 6:23). This focus on heaven and an afterlife may also have been an unusual feature: the Sadducees denied the existence of an afterlife, while the Pharisees seemed to have only a hazy notion of it. It may suggest, however, that the early optimism had faded and been replaced with a realisation that the kingdom would arrive on the earth only with great effort, considerable sacrifice and much suffering. Many who paid this price might never see the kingdom arrive on earth at all and would need the assurance of some compensation elsewhere.

The Gospel writers do not give us any indication of a progression of ideas in Jesus's teaching, except that near the end he seemed to accept the fact that his own death was inevitable and would, in some mysterious way, open the way for a new relationship between humankind and God. Perhaps Jesus was so convinced of the rewards to be had in the afterlife that even death by crucifixion seemed to be a price worth paying. To assume that Jesus's message did undergo a change of emphasis would appear to make more sense than attempting to reconcile apparently conflicting ideas that may have existed at different periods of his ministry.

Unfortunately, the early kingdom ideals of Jesus seem to be at odds not only with human nature in general but even with redeemed human nature. No such society has existed for any length of time. Among any group of people living together in community, there are always those who are leaders and those who are content to be led, and time will inevitably produce a hierarchy and a structured organisation. Those who gravitate to the top of any hierarchy seem to have a peculiar and unfortunate knack of separating themselves from the common herd at the earliest opportunity, although Jesus himself could never be accused of such conduct.

Jesus's power of communication is demonstrated by the parables he told, many of which are unsurpassed for their simplicity and beauty. Perhaps we lose some of their cutting edge because of our familiarity with them and our unfamiliarity with the times in which Jesus lived. The impact of the story of the Good Samaritan may be better appreciated if we were to imagine a Jewish Rabbi today telling the story of a Good Palestinian to an audience of Ultra-Zionists, or a Presbyterian minister in Belfast talking about a Good Roman Catholic to a crowd of loyalist paramilitaries.

There can be few parents who cannot empathise with the father in the story of the Prodigal (lost) Son, and few who cannot imagine the anxiety of a shepherd who has lost one of his sheep. The parables of the lost sheep and the prodigal son, together with the Good Samaritan, must be three of the most famous stories ever told. It is rather surprising, therefore, to find that apart from Luke's Gospel where all three parables are recorded, the other only mention of any of them, the lost sheep, comes in Matthew's Gospel and also in the non-canonical gospel of Thomas.

One mark of real genius, however, lies in the ability to simplify all the complexities of life into something short, clear and easily digestible. Jesus excelled in this area. Asked on one occasion what he considered to be the greatest of all commandments (Matthew 22:35-40), he replies by apparently giving not one commandment, as asked, but two. However, maybe the most important one is "*You shall love your neighbour as you love yourself.*" Jesus precedes this with the commandment about loving God with all your heart, with all your soul, with all your strength and with all your mind, possibly because he knew that in a religious society, regard for one's neighbour would be dependent on regard for one's God. In Mark 2:27 Jesus makes a remarkable statement which amplifies this when he says "*The Sabbath was made for man, not man for the Sabbath.*" This is tantamount to saying that all the commandments were made for the benefit of men, not for the benefit of God.

The God that Jesus presented may desire our love, but he wants this to be a matter of the heart and not in any way to be turned into something that is an onerous duty. Since God does not actually need anything, the needs of human beings are at the centre of real religion. And furthermore, loving one's neighbour means "*do to others what you would have them do to you*" (Matt 7:12). This statement apparently has variations in many societies going back to before the time of Jesus. In Jesus's own day, the Rabbi Hillel said: "*Do not do to others what you would not wish them to do to you.*"

Jesus, however, changes this negative statement to a positive command. There is a huge difference between the two.

There is one last point that must be made. Jesus does seem to have had a reputation as a healer. We cannot be sure what form this took, but it seems to have impressed many people of his day. There is the suggestion of the effect of an immensely powerful personality upon the recipients in some cases, as if something akin to the well-known placebo effect of today was in operation. In the end, however, we are left with a feeling of bafflement, because many of the things that are supposed to have occurred are quite simply outside our modern day experience. Given the fact that Luke says great miracles were not uncommon in the early Church, we can either assume that this is wild exaggeration, pure invention, or else we can try and explain why such miracles do not seem to happen in our own time.

There is no shortage of people who have attempted the latter. In view of what has already been said about two particular miracles in John's Gospel, I am now convinced that what we have is a mixture of gross exaggeration and invention in the written accounts and that the Holy Spirit, who apparently bestowed upon the disciple these miraculous powers was, in fact, nothing more than a figment of Jesus's imagination and is now a figment of our own imaginations.

The death of Jesus gives rise to fewer problems than most other aspects of Jesus's life, although there are one or two issues, beginning with the arrest of Jesus in the Garden of Gethsemane. All the Gospels mention an incident in which a follower of Jesus cuts off the ear of a servant of the High Priest, John saying that it was Simon Peter. Luke however, who has already mentioned that two of Jesus's disciples were armed with swords (Luke 22:38) also mentions that his followers asked him (v 49) "*Lord, should we strike with our swords?*"

Why would any of Jesus's followers be carrying swords? Would not this be a dangerous thing to do in a Jerusalem with Roman soldiers on the look-out for potential trouble-makers and obsessed, as they would be, with the possibility of armed insurrection from Jews in a state of heightened, religious excitement? Did the disciples harbour the secret belief that Jesus was going to cause an uprising and they wished to be ready for such an event? Were they anticipating the arrival of the kingdom that Jesus had talked about? Did they always carry such weapons as a necessary means of self-defence in a lawless country? Such a situation would suggest that their faith in God, and indeed, Jesus's faith in God, was not all that it we imagine it to have been. Swords have one purpose only—to inflict injury or death on another human being, even if that is done is self-defence. It does seem so utterly out of character with everything Jesus stood for. Unfortunately, we do not know the answer to these questions. They are just another conundrum in a sea of similar conundrums that make up the Gospels.

All the Gospels agree that Jesus was executed by the Romans, although they all lay the ultimate blame for his death on the Jewish authorities. Roman executions by crucifixion were barbaric in the extreme. Pilate is said to have ordered an inscription to be put on the cross of Jesus to the effect that he was the King of the Jews. Pilate is unlikely to have had much sympathy for any victim, however innocent, and his action could only have been to show the Jews that this is how Romans would treat Jewish kings not of their own appointment. He would certainly have had every reason for wishing to eliminate the remotest possible threat from any potential Jewish leader. Crucifixions were carried out not only to punish individuals but also to suppress the population. Jesus would have been crucified where nearly all the pilgrims to the city that day would see him. One image of this kind, without doubt, would have more effect in suppressing a potentially rebellious people than a thousand threats would have had.

There are six recorded utterances that Jesus is said to have made from the cross. One we have already referred to in connection with the Virgin Birth. I will refer to just two further utterances. The first is in Luke 23:34 where Jesus says: "*Father, forgive them, for they know not what they do*" If Jesus did say this, it must rank as the greatest saying ever to be uttered by any human being. Indeed, the manner in which Jesus appeared to endure this suffering may have left an indelible impression with the disciples, further distancing him, in their minds, from the common herd or the rest of society. Did his apparent acceptance of his fate further convince them of the fact that he was different in some remarkable way, and did this make a major contribution to the ultimate understanding of him as the Son of God?

The second utterance is in Matthew 27:45, where he says: "*My God, my God, why have you forsaken me*?" Could this possibly have been the cry of a man who had not expected things to end like this, the cry of a man who felt abandoned and whose faith vanished, even if only momentarily, in a time of extreme suffering and bewilderment?

It is recorded that the body of Jesus was granted to Joseph of Arimathea. Actual details of crucifixions are in short supply, although there is a heel bone, discovered in an ancient Jewish cemetery in 1968 that has a nail driven through it. Extracting the nail from the bone must have proved too difficult a task, although this should not necessarily be a cause for surprise. Even extracting the nail from the wood would have been difficult enough as this process usually requires some means of providing leverage of the kind available with a hammer and claw. With any part of the body between the head of the nail and the wood, the operation would be impossible without causing huge further damage to these body parts. It is certainly not a process that would have left the neat, small wounds depicted in certain classical paintings.

The Romans would have been concerned with putting bodies on crosses in such a way that they stayed there, not with the ease of removing them later on. Indeed, it would almost certainly have been in their interest to use nails that were designed to make the removal of a body as difficult as possible. Should they themselves have wished to remove any body from a cross, the easiest option would have been to chop off the hands (arms) and feet first.

University of Texas biblical scholar, L. Michael White, who participated in a study of crucifixions, is convinced that nobody who had undergone crucifixion would ever be able to walk again as a result of damage caused to the bones by the crucifixion process. This calls into question the authenticity of the narrative of a physically resurrected Jesus inviting Thomas to put his fingers into the wounds to dispel his doubts, as if he was still in his crucified body (John 20:27). Exactly what connection Jesus's resurrected body had to his crucified body is yet another conundrum.

It is the story of the burial, however, where differences of detail give rise to the suspicion that the story may have been tampered with. John, in contrast to the synoptic Gospel accounts, tells us that Nicodemus accompanied Joseph of Arimathea in burying Jesus and that Nicodemus had a considerable quantity of spices with him in order to anoint the body according to the Jewish custom. John further tells us that they placed Jesus's body in a nearby tomb, because "*it was the Jewish day of Preparation.*" The technical difficulties involved with this phrase are too complex to discuss here. I will simply assume that we are talking about Friday and the Jewish Sabbath (day of rest) was about to begin. John does not say that the tomb where Jesus was placed belonged to Joseph. It simply provided a convenient location in the circumstances, a point that we shall return to later.

13   WHO MOVED THE STONE?

There is one remaining issue to be addressed before we conclude this study of the enigma that is Jesus. If we suppose that there may not have been a physical resurrection, is there any way that we can we account for the fact that a movement with a small number of up-country adherents, whose leader had been executed in a manner suggesting rejection by God (Deuteronomy 21:23), not only survived but continued to grow? Frank Morrison (real name Albert Henry Ross) was the author of an extremely influential book, *Who Moved the Stone?* first published in 1930, and he clearly did not believe so. His arguments in favour of a physical resurrection focussed on three main points: the empty tomb, the failure of anyone to produce a dead body and the astonishing boldness of the disciples in proclaiming the Resurrection a short time afterwards.

I read his book when I was at university as it was recommended reading for all Christian Union members, and one very prominent evangelist recommended it not too long ago at the church that I used to attend. It still seems to be widely read and I have to admit that it made a big impression on me when I read it. However, I am now convinced that there is an alternative explanation for the survival of the Jesus movement, one that does not require a physically resurrected Jesus. It should be remembered, in any case, that the change in the disciples was not produced as a result of the Resurrection but by the coming of the Holy Spirit at Pentecost.

Two factors certainly would have had to be present for the disciples to have come to believe that Jesus had indeed risen from the dead. The first is that the personality of Jesus must have been so extraordinarily powerful that not even his horrendous death could extinguish the influence of his life and his message. In fact, his death must have triggered a fierce determination among his followers to maintain his memory alive in view of what subsequently happened. The second is that the message itself contained a vision that was so appealing that his followers could not let go of it. Beyond this, other factors no doubt also played a part, some of which are discussed in what follows.

I think back to the young African preacher that I mentioned in my first book, Manasseh Mankuleiyo, whom I witnessed preaching to several thousand people in a Nairobi park in the early 1970s. He was a shepherd with a large following of sheep. They followed him because he preached a message that gave them hope and purpose and certainty. He preached a message that recognised the reality of their present circumstances but offered a vision of a better future and a chance to taste a little bit of heaven here on earth, the love of God that produces love between men.

I sometimes wondered what would have happened if Manasseh had suddenly met a violent death because his message was deemed a threat to the political establishment or because he happened to be from the "wrong" tribe. Would his following simply have disappeared into thin air? Or would the vision that he gave to people survive and he himself continue to occupy an exalted position in their hearts? Manasseh was a shepherd who had his own sheep. Jesus was the Good Shepherd, the shepherd *par excellence.* Would not his sheep continue in the way that he had taught them and would they not venerate his memory? And if they did so, would not their view of him become more exalted with the passage of time? I am not at all convinced that it wouldn't.

However, we need to start with the situation immediately following the death of Jesus. We are told that Joseph of Arimathea, a rich resident of Judea, placed the body in a near-by tomb. The Gospels are unanimous on this point but only Matthew says that Joseph was the owner of the tomb. The Gospels are also unanimous that the tomb was empty on the Sunday morning. The burial, which occurred on Friday evening, was immediately followed by a period of enforced rest for the Jewish Sabbath and this meant that nothing could have happened, in practice, until Saturday evening, at the end of the Sabbath. This would have afforded the disciples some time, in reasonable safety, to take stock of their grim situation.

It may be that they were very uncertain. They must have reflected on the recent events of the Last Supper and on the Mount of Olives, where Jesus is said not only to have foretold his immanent death but also, according to two of the Gospels, the fact that he would rise and go ahead of them into Galilee (Matthew 26:32; Mark 14:28). If this was the case, then, given the fact that they could easily have imagined that their own lives might be in danger once Sunday arrived, they would have had every incentive to plan a rapid departure back to Galilee at the earliest possible opportunity, in other words, early on the Sunday morning

I will now return to the account of the empty tomb found in John's Gospel, which I believe has more than a hint of truth about it. John implies that Mary Magdalene went to the tomb alone and not to anoint the body, because this had already been done by Nicodemus on the Friday evening (John 19:38-42). There is only one explanation of why she would do this, ignoring the danger that an attractive, unaccompanied woman might have been exposed to and risking suspicion and scandal by her action. She had been in love with Jesus and simply had to be near his grave, preferably alone. It is one of the strongest impulses in the human psyche. All those who have buried loved ones know the pull of the grave. My wife and I return again and again to the grave of our dead child. The issue of the stone was not relevant. She did not want to do anything with the body; she just wanted to be there.

The writer of this Gospel must have been fairly well acquainted with Mary and thought sufficient of her to record what really happened, to give her a place in posterity. In so doing, he exalted the position of women forever. Jesus, according to John, chose to make the greatest revelation ever accorded to a human being to a woman. If Luke's story of the Incarnation is one of the most beautiful ever told, then John's story of Mary's supposed meeting with Jesus in the garden must rank alongside it. It tells of a thrilling, uplifting, emotionally charged encounter, and it pulsates with new life, restored hope and human love. The brief drama reaches its climax with just one word, but a word with sufficient potency to transform her life forever: "*Mary.*" Jesus speaks her name and the world stops still while the most unimaginable feelings must have flooded her being. Sadly, the story then ends in an anti-climax. Mary's love remains unrequited: she is not allowed to hold on to Jesus. Maybe he is not actually there, except in her imagination, her dreams and her heart, where he would remain to her dying day.

This story, I suspect, gets closest to what probably did happen. Most likely Mary was the first to visit the tomb, very early in the morning. Discovering the tomb to be empty with the stone rolled back, she dashed back to the disciples and then returned to the tomb with Peter and John. The detail that she then remained behind weeping after they had left has an authentic ring to it. Who cannot empathise with this poor, distraught woman? The encounter with Jesus would not have occurred here, but there is every reason to believe that she dreamt of such a meeting in the nights that followed.

This Gospel may have been the last to be written, but it might have swept aside the proclivities of the age and restored the uncensored version for us. For censored versions there seem to have been, versions that removed the scandalous suggestion that Jesus could ever have provoked this kind of love in a woman. And so, for the sake of decency, the other Gospels include other women to accompany Mary Magdalene to the grave. Mark and Luke even add a plausible reason for these actions and hence are obliged to remove the part that John says Nicodemus played in the story. All of this, I suspect, was merely a cosmetic exercise in deference to the sensibilities of the day.

Mary cannot have been privy to any promise of Jesus to rise again and make an appearance to his disciples in Galilee. She was also totally unprepared for what she discovered—an empty tomb. If the disciples had had even the slimmest hope of a resurrection, would not the very fact of an empty tomb have lifted their expectations? Even with no prior expectation, they would have been puzzled. It would be relatively easy for their gullible and superstitious minds to imagine all sorts of possibilities. However, there would not have been anything to gain by trying to investigate the matter any further. Jesus had said he would see them in Galilee, but even without this promise, every unnecessary moment spent in or around Jerusalem could prove costly. If the leader had fared as he had, would his closest disciples be exempt from danger? For the safety of all, a hasty evacuation back to Galilee was, without doubt, the most sensible option available to them. The empty tomb would have to remain unexplained, but it must have triggered some uncertainty, and possibly hope, within them. Could it be that Jesus had, in some unfathomable way, been able to overcome death?

The only realistic explanation for an empty tomb is that Joseph and Nicodemus had had the body removed and reburied elsewhere. This is not unreasonable, particularly if the tomb did not belong to Joseph. Who knows if any permission to use the tomb was ever granted? The narratives, except for Matthew, do not suggest that it was. And if not, it would be imperative to remove the body at the earliest possible opportunity, at the end of the Sabbath on Saturday evening. If this happened, and a hasty reburial was made in semi-darkness, it could have occurred at an unmarked spot. The location of that spot may not have been precisely known once signs of the fresh movement of earth had faded. It is even possible that the body was deliberately placed in an inconspicuous location. For these two men, whatever their devotion to Jesus had been, their sorrow must have been tinged with bitter disappointment. Jesus, like other would-be leaders before him, had promised much but his life had clearly ended in tragic failure. To allow his body to rest in peace, to let his memory fade, was perhaps the kindest service that they could now afford him.

As for the followers of Jesus, undertaking a hurried retreat from Jerusalem, a desperate hope that Jesus might, in fact, have come back to life could have been born within them. After all, they were, by and large, ignorant, superstitious, incredulous peasants. If they did have any expectation in this regard, it is more than possible that they would have all remained together as a group, even when they reached the safety of Galilee. If there was even the remotest possibility that Jesus was alive and hence might appear to them, they would all want to be there together to witness the event.

They would, however, still be traumatised, and in a state of mixed, heightened emotions. The horror of the crucifixion must have been deeply etched in their minds. They would have been physically as well as emotionally exhausted at the end of a long, hastily executed journey. When, during the nights, sleep eventually overwhelmed them, they would inevitably dream. And the conditions were highly conducive to their having dreams of meeting with a risen Jesus.

We now have to remember that dreams in those days had a much greater significance than most people attach to them today. Dreams were the means by which God, or his angels, communicated important things to human beings. When Joseph was in prison in Egypt, Pharaoh had dreams which troubled him but which

Joseph was able to interpret as a heavenly warning. When God needed to communicate some important news about a virgin girl called Mary to another Joseph over a thousand years later, he used a dream. Peter was to recall a prophecy in Joel 2:28: "*In the last days God says, I will pour out my Spirit on all people. Your sons and daughters will prophesy, your young men will* **see visions***, your old men will* **dream dreams***. Even on my servants, both men and women, I will pour out my Spirit in those days and they will prophesy*" (Acts 2:17-18 [emphasis added]).

If many of them had similar dreams, and possibly more than one dream each, what significance would they attach to them? Is it not likely that they might see these dreams as a fulfilment of Jesus's promise to appear to them? Dreams alone would not have sufficed to convince them of a physical resurrection. However, dreams coupled with an empty tomb, in the superstitious age in which they lived, may well have done. Furthermore, dreams of this kind would eventually fade away, just as the resurrection appearances seemed to fade away, and would do so without unnecessary, accompanying dreams of an ascension, which may explain why three of the Gospels do not mention it. If such dreams did form a part of their belief in a resurrection, it is not surprising that it has never been possible to construct any coherent sequence to the events surrounding the resurrection appearances.

However, the sharing of such dreams must have added another dimension to their emotional state. If, as good Jews, they were also in the habit of praising God in worship, they could have arrived at a point where emotional outbursts spontaneously broke forth, possibly with uncontrolled babbling. If this did happen, it would surely have been seen as a further fulfilment of Joel's prophecy concerning the outpouring of God's Spirit.

I have a vivid recollection in my own life of a dream induced by an overwrought state of mind. I was on leave, having finished a three year period in Uganda, a period ending with a severe bout of malaria from which I found it difficult to recover. The issue of the "Baptism with the Holy Spirit" had begun to occupy my mind a great deal. I had been dissatisfied with my first three years in Uganda. I believed that there had to be something more and that this experience might supply the key and provide what so far appeared to have been missing. I had talked about the experience with some Pentecostal missionaries from Germany who lived in the nearby town, but I had never quite seemed able to enter into the experience myself.

There is no doubt that I became completely obsessed with the issue, reading every book that I could find on the subject and spending time in prayer and seeking God. Then, one night, I suddenly began babbling away, making unknown sounds as I was swept into some sort of ecstatic state. Words gushed forth and I was unable to stop them. So intense was the experience that I suddenly felt unable to breathe and feared that I would die if the experience did not stop. Stop it suddenly did when I woke up. I had been dreaming. It was the only time that I ever had an experience of this intensity, even if it was not, in fact, real.

Had I actually been "Baptised in the Spirit?" I do not know. When I returned to Uganda, it was with considerably more success than I had experienced during my first tour. Revival was in the air and the Gospel began to take centre stage. I even began to preach and see people converted. Miracles, however, continued to be elusive. Whatever the truth, my dream shows what can happen when we are unable to get something out of our minds. The disciples must have been in a state of mind that would have rendered them prone to vivid dreams about the traumatic events that they had so recently lived through.

The experience that I had in a dream, I have witnessed others have in reality. Some people who partake in an emotional form of group worship are prone to what I can only describe as emotional hysteria where all control is lost and uncontrolled babbling ensues. They are often encouraged to believe that this is the experience called the baptism with the Holy Spirit. There are those who appear able to enter such a state of emotional ecstasy quite easily. Did the disciples experience something such as this as they prayed and worshipped together? Could this have been the origin of their belief that this was the promised Holy Spirit that Jesus had spoken of?

If dreams and emotional experiences did occur within the group, the conviction that Jesus had indeed risen and that God was inaugurating a new era could easily have taken root. Furthermore, the empty tomb would have to be explained. If Jesus had risen, then what became of him? The obvious answer is that he went to be reunited with his Father in heaven. That meant some sort of ascension into heaven in the eyes of the disciples. There could easily have been a vague belief that this is what must have occurred, but it was not an event that anybody witnessed, or, apparently, even dreamed about. Thus three Gospels make no specific reference to an actual ascension event. Luke, the expert mythologist, is the only one to grasp the nettle and include the event in his narrative.

Galilee, where Jesus had been a prominent figure, is more much likely to have provided the fertile soil necessary for the new movement to flourish. It seems much more likely that the early Church had its beginnings here and then spread outwards, and that the disciples did not return to Jerusalem for some considerable time, certainly not while the death of Jesus remained in any way a raw, emotive issue.

When some of them did venture to visit Jerusalem again for one of the festivals, and judged it feasible to preach their message, the issue surrounding the missing body may not have been relevant. A body that could be identified as that of Jesus could no longer be produced. Other crucifixions would have taken place and other bodies been buried. Who could prove that any decayed body was that of Jesus? The exact location of Jesus's body may no longer have been known for certain. In any case, the disciples were already fully convinced that he had risen. They had seen him, even if it was only in their dreams, and God had apparently poured out his Spirit. The Resurrection, for them, was an article of faith. Personal experience would take precedence over objective facts if ever there was a conflict, a situation that most evangelicals ought to recognise quite easily: "*We know what we have believed*" is the rallying cry of many a pastor.

As for Joseph and Nicodemus and any others involved in the final interment of Jesus's body, would they try to locate it to verify for themselves if Jesus really could have risen? Such a thing may no longer have been possible, but in any case, if his disciples had seen him, then there could not be any doubt. Also, people who desperately want to believe in something do not usually seek out evidence that might negate those beliefs. Such procedures belong to the world of science and neither Joseph nor Nicodemus were scientists. They were would-be believers and almost certainly gullible and superstitious. It is, of course, possible that neither of them was still alive.

We cannot say exactly what message the disciples first began to preach, but it seems that baptism in water was re-introduced (it had been a feature of Jesus's early ministry according to John's Gospel). However, there was now a different emphasis. Baptism for the forgiveness of sins was performed *"in the name of Jesus Christ."* Jesus's original message of the kingdom would probably have had a central place but with a new twist. Many people were still living in anticipation of the kingdom. Joseph of Arimathea was said to be one such person according to both Mark and Luke (Mark 15:43; Luke 23:51). But the message the disciples proclaimed was different: the kingdom was no longer "at hand"; it had arrived! Jesus had promised it and in some mysterious way, his death had opened the way for God to bring it about in the here and now. Jesus would be presented as the promised Messiah. His resurrection, together with the new experience of the Holy Spirit, would be the God-given guarantee that he (God) had inaugurated the kingdom.

Early gatherings would probably have centred around the custom that Jesus introduced at the last supper, now known as the Eucharist or the Holy Communion, and would have included ecstatic worship and speaking in tongues. It would have been be novel and mysterious, two ingredients that are always likely to attract followers, and probably they had little trouble doing so among the Galilean peasants. Novelty in religion may have been as exciting as life ever got for many of them.

Since it remained a Jewish movement, the message could not have been as full-bloodied as Peter's supposed address on the day of Pentecost. It must have accommodated itself, however uneasily, within traditional Judaism. This was a new Jewish sect that believed that the Messiah had come and the kingdom had been inaugurated and was being established. Traditional Jews continued to look for a future Messiah and a future kingdom. Somehow, they managed to co-exist. But it was not the Gospel as Paul eventually came to understand it and as evangelical Christians understand it today. Friction and conflict did occur between the new movement and the more traditional Jews and persecution occasionally erupted, but the new movement was not destroyed.

The situation may not have been very different from what has occurred throughout Church history, particularly after the Reformation, and there has been evidence of a similar situation in very recent times. When the message of the Pentecostal Church began to filter into mainstream churches, those accepting the new ideas became known as charismatics. For a long while they remained in their individual denominational churches, and some have continued to do so. However, tensions arose, and in many cases the inevitable eventually happened. Some charismatics left those churches where they felt frustrated or no longer welcome and banded together with charismatics from other churches to form new, independent church groups. They were originally known as the House Church movement as, having no buildings of their own, they met in each other's houses, an exact duplication of the situation that existed in the early Church. With time, many of these groups have developed into major churches with membership far exceeding that of most traditional churches, and often believing that they alone represent the real Church of God. The charismatic element among those who chose to remain faithful to their denominations often faded away, although there are a number of Anglican clergy who would claim to be charismatic and run charismatic Anglican churches. However, the overall result is often what might be expected when putting new wine into old wineskins. There is little resemblance, certainly between the often insipid worship of the traditionalists and the passion found in the independent and truly charismatic Churches.

In the end, there is no way of knowing with absolute certainty what really happened on that fateful weekend nearly two thousand years ago. We just know that sometime soon afterwards, Christianity was born and survived. This scenario I have given may not seem likely but it seems to me that this, or something similar, has every bit as much credibility as the story that the Bible itself tells. It also explains the existence of the empty tomb, the failure of the authorities to produce a body and the transformation that occurred in the disciples. In other words it answers all the main arguments in Frank Morrison's book *Who Moved the Stone?*

14 THE INFLUENCE OF ST PAUL

St. Paul's appearance on the scene was a decisive turning point in the history of the fledgling Jesus movement. Paul, on his own later admission, was a fanatical adherent of traditional Judaism. Fanaticism is one manifestation of an unsatisfied hunger for something not already in one's possession. If you want the truth and don't feel content with what you have so far acquired, you are driven to greater efforts in pursuit of it. No stone can be left unturned in your determination to find answers.

Great, world changing discoveries in science are never made by people who are satisfied with whatever knowledge and understanding they already possess. They are made by people who realise that what they know is not the whole truth, that somewhere there must be a more satisfying explanation, a deeper truth. They are made by people who are fanatical in their desire to know the deepest truths about the whys and wherefores of the natural world.

Circumstances no doubt determined that Paul's considerable intellectual abilities and energy would be directed to the issue of religion, Jewish religion. He does not appear to have been born in a place where his restless mind was exposed to the ideas of philosophy or science that might have circulated amongst the more Hellenised citizens of the Roman Empire. It seems clear, however, in view of Paul's later life, that Judaism could not have provided him with the satisfaction he sought.

Something must have been missing or some things did not quite add up. Circumstances, at some point, brought him into contact with the Jesus movement and something about this sect upset him, so much so that he violently opposed it. Fanaticism can never tolerate even small differences of opinion.

Unfortunately, we have no real knowledge of how Paul acquired his version of Christianity. He refuses to acknowledge any debt to other human beings, even though Luke says that he was present when Stephen was stoned and would therefore have acquired some knowledge of what Christians believed from this incident, if, of course, it ever took place. Unfortunately, Luke's credibility is virtually non-existent when it comes to his narrative and so we cannot take anything for granted.

Paul's Gospel, if we are to believe him, was conveyed to him directly from heaven. More probably, after some eureka moment, he studied the scriptures and from these emerged his own, possibly unique, brand of the faith. There is no evidence that he sought, or needed, the approval of the original disciples for anything that he preached or subsequently wrote. This presents us with tantalising possibilities. Did Paul add new dimensions to the original apostolic message? Was his understanding changed in any way when he took the Gospel to the Gentiles? Did he pre-empt the disciples by being the first to commit his ideas to writing?

We do know that Paul forced at least one issue on the early Church, that of circumcision (Acts chapter 15). Removal of this requirement for Gentile believers opened a fissure in the movement that led, eventually, to complete rupture. This probably occurred after the fall of Jerusalem in 70 CE, following the Jewish rebellion against Rome. What we do know is that it was Paul's Gentile Gospel that survived. The Jewish version of Christianity was lost and we have no idea how it differed from the Gospel that we know today.

Paul's letters, rather like John's Gospel, concentrate on the person and redeeming work of Jesus. The world of both John and Paul is no longer divided into Jews and Gentiles. It is divided into those who believe and accept the claim that Jesus was the Son of God, and those who reject that claim. Perhaps we ought to add a third group of those who have never heard the Gospel. The disciples may have been confused but not Paul apparently. It leaves us wondering whether Paul brought a lot of clarity to the muddled ideas that may have existed at the start. Just how much clarity did he bring? Would the Gospel be the same as it is today if Paul had never lived? Indeed, would there have been any Church at all if he had not lived?

We have already noted that Paul's explanation of the cause of homosexuality is at odds not only with nearly all scientific medical opinion but also with most of the information that I collected over many months, most of that from gay or lesbian practising Christians. There are two other areas of Paul's teachings that had given me niggling doubts over a number of years: his views on the Second Coming of Jesus and his views on women.

The problem with the first of these two issues is that Paul, in common with all the other Christians of his day, clearly expected Jesus to return to the earth next month, if not next week, abolish the present order and usher in the kingdom of God in all its totality. He was so sure of the immanent return of Jesus that he advised people that it would be better for an unmarried man "*not to look for a wife*" (1 Corinthians 7:27). The reason for this is given in verse 29: "*What I mean, brothers, is that the time is short.*" Too little time, presumably, for it to be worth anyone's while to think of getting married as there would not be sufficient time to produce children and raise families.

Paul did not forbid marriage, but he definitely did not encourage it, and on grounds that turned out to be false. I have often wondered how many people's lives were denied one of the great pleasures of our existence because they followed that advice. That is not to say that marriage is essential to happiness. I was perfectly happy as a single person. But to fall in love, and then not to carry that emotion through to its natural conclusion, and for a reason that was simply wrong, seems to me to be rather tragic, and not something to be laid at the door of God the Father or the Holy Spirit.

The other issue that I had with Paul's writings is in regard to his belief about the status of women. In 1 Corinthians 14:33-35, we read: "*As in all the congregations of the saints, women should remain silent in the churches. They are not allowed to speak, but must be in submission, as the Law says. If they want to enquire about something, they should ask their own husbands at home; for it is disgraceful for a woman to speak in the church.*" In other words, women were to be silent when men were present because they were somehow spiritually inferior, if not just inferior per se. In chapter 11 we are told that they were allowed to pray and prophesy, presumably in women's only meetings, providing they had their heads covered.

Paul may have had a distorted view of a woman's place in the world, just as he seems to have been strangely preoccupied with the fashions of his day, the adornments worn by women and the length of people's hair not escaping his attention. However, I have taught many girls in my time and a good number of them have been extremely able. I have also taught some boys who certainly found my subject, physics, to be very challenging. Paul could never have imagined such a thing because girls received no formal education in the Jewish society of his day.

If a girl can have a level of intelligence far superior to that of many boys, why should we imagine that this could not apply in spiritual matters? There is no good reason and hence no reason why women should accept second class citizenship in matters of religion. It is nothing more than a matter of tradition that originated in primitive societies. These views of Paul are often waved away with the explanation that they are cultural issues. That, however, is precisely the problem, for it is an admission that the Bible is a product of the culture in which it was produced and therefore can make no claim to represent timeless truth. The God of the Bible is a God who changes not (Malachi 3:6). The Holy Spirit, one presumes, would not have been restricted by such cultural mores or lack of knowledge or indeed encumbered by any kind of prejudice. Paul, however, was hampered by all these matters. He wrote from his own very limited perspective. It has to be conceded that Paul's views about women seem to be far closer to the Islamic views that are prevalent in a number of

Muslim societies and, indeed, among a not insignificant number of Muslims in our own society, than to anything that people with a modern, western education would accept.

Perhaps I should not be so hard on St. Paul. He was in many ways a very great man and he certainly achieved incredible things in his lifetime. It is Paul, more than any other person that we know of, who was responsible for the spread of Christianity into the western Gentile world, and his writings have left an indelible mark on Christian doctrine and Church practice. For all that, however, he was also clearly a man of his time. And in St. Paul's time, there was not a great deal of knowledge to be had, certainly not if you were a Jew that despised the godless Gentile world and all that it stood for. And there was no knowledge at all of the realities of human sexuality.

The Greeks had produced many wonderful writers, philosophers, scientists and mathematicians by the time Paul lived. Homer had written his great works, Socrates, Plato and Aristotle, the great philosophers, had all been and gone. Pythagoras, Euclid and Archimedes, names that ought to be familiar to every schoolboy and schoolgirl, had also been and gone. Eratosthenes, not quite so well known, had not only realised that the Earth was a sphere, but by a staggering piece of reasoning and mathematics, had managed to work out a value for its circumference, one that is very close to the value accepted today. All this, incidentally, occurred over three hundred years before Jesus was born.

However, this kind of knowledge was not likely to have been very widespread in its time and it would definitely not be in the realm of Jewish thought.

Knowledge and understanding to a Jew meant only one thing—knowledge of their Scriptures, more or less what we know now as the Old Testament. Beyond that there would have been superstition, beliefs lacking any credible evidence for their existence. The knowledge that the Greeks had brought to the world was to disappear from Western Europe when Christianity became the dominant religion and was only preserved because early Islamic culture seemed to value knowledge more highly than its Christian counterpart did.

In the days of Paul, anything that did not have an obvious explanation would be explained in terms of his religious beliefs. This was not, of course, something that was peculiar to Jews and Judaism. Most people of the period attributed events on earth to the activities of the gods. To offend the gods was to invite punishment, and much time was spent in trying to ensure that a god's displeasure was not aroused. It should hardly be surprising, therefore, to find that Paul blames what he would have seen as the curse of homosexuality on man having offended his (Paul's) God in one way or another.

Paul did not inhabit a world of scientific evidence or extensive knowledge. His was a world where everything that happened in life was a consequence of man's relationship to, and obedience to, the one true God. So, in the matter of homosexuality, he advanced the only explanation that it was possible for him to do, the only one that made any sense to him. That a large group of Christians today should choose to his elevate his opinions above those of modern science does little credit to them.

The written accounts in the Old Testament are an accumulation of writings, possibly done over several centuries, but it is very likely that the only written copies would have been kept in the royal archives or in the temple at Jerusalem. Both 2 Kings 22 and 2 Chronicles 34 contain accounts of the finding of the "Book of the Law" during a refurbishment of the temple in the eighteenth year of King Josiah's reign. However, it transpires that the reading of this book shocked Josiah because its contents were apparently new to him.

One possibility is that written documents were not plentiful in the time of Josiah. In fact, Josiah's grandfather, Manasseh, who had reigned for 55 years (the longest reign of any king of Judah) was not noted for his devotion to the God of his people and is unlikely to have made any effort to maintain a library of Jewish religious works. A second possibility is that the priests in the temple wrote this document themselves and presented it to Josiah in the hope that his reforming zeal might be directed in ways they that they themselves approved of. It is certainly a reasonably strong possibility that very few and possibly no documents relating to Jewish history or the Jewish religion would have made it to Babylon after the destruction of Jerusalem and the temple by the Babylonian army in 587 BCE.

If this was the case, a complete Old Testament may well have had to be compiled from scratch during and after the Babylonian captivity. It was possibly not finished until the near the beginning of the first century BCE. This would allow the writers to influence the content to reflect their own particular ideas and these would in turn be influenced by the circumstances of the times in which they wrote. They would also be writing several hundred years after some of the major events they described were supposed to have occurred. Indeed, the record of Moses' life and achievements ends by claiming: "*Since then, no prophet has arisen in Israel like Moses*" (Deuteronomy 34:10), suggesting that a considerable period had elapsed between the events described and the written recording of them. And, of course, it is always much easier to talk about miracles that occurred in some far-off time. They can no longer be disputed. Miracles, as we have already noted, always seem to be events that occur in faraway places or distant times or both of these. People who have never seen a miracle occur in their own church, and never expect to see one, do not seem to have any difficulty believing in tremendous miracles that are apparently occurring somewhere in California or Florida.

It is also likely that the entire Jewish canon was ultimately the work of the Babylonian Jewish community and their descendants. When a number of them were allowed to return to Jerusalem under an edict of the Persian king, Cyrus the Great, they do not appear to have welcomed outsiders, even if these outsiders may have originally been bona fide Jews who were occupying the territory prior to the return of the deportees. In the Book of Ezra we are confronted with a fanatical priest obsessed with the blood purity of the people, an intolerant racist *par excellence*. Non-Jewish wives were to be got rid of. There was to be a new start, a new people for a new city, and over the years to come, no doubt, new Scriptures that would further define their Jewishness. Was the entire Pentateuch, containing the great epic story of the Exodus, actually inspired by deliberations on their experience of captivity in Babylon and their subsequent deliverance? It is hardly likely, under these circumstances, that Jews who had escaped to Egypt rather than been deported to Babylon, for instance, would have been allowed to have any input to the new order.

To understand how a document as vast as the Old Testament came into being at all, we perhaps need to understand the role of the story-teller in the ancient world. With no television, radio, books or any other of the ready-made forms of entertainment that we rely on today, story-telling would have been a prime source of entertainment and gifted story-tellers would have been hugely popular. The art of great story-telling lies in the ability to provide embellishment on a factual skeleton or even a totally fictional one.

One of my uncles was a great story-teller. I am told that he rarely had to buy his own beer. Others kept him well plied just to listen to his stories. They had heard most of them before but there were always new embellishments. He would often entertain us as young children and his stories were as funny as they were far-fetched. Each time he told them there would be differences, some new addition or new twist to the tale. I have one abiding memory of him. My elder brother and I were visiting our grandparents and our uncle was there discussing horses with granddad. Granddad liked an occasional, and usually unsuccessful, flutter on the horses (or gee-gees as he called them) when he had a spare shilling (probably worth about 50p in modern currency). Neither my brother nor I knew anything about racehorses but we did know all about carthorses (also known as shire horses) used in the fields or for pulling heavy carts laden with beer barrels. My elder brother asked if there was a difference between racehorses and carthorses. My uncle gave him a look of great consternation and replied "*Aye, there is that, son. Them are carthorses that your granddad keeps putting his money on.*" He died at the age of forty-nine, before the dangers of smoking and heavy drinking were fully appreciated. He was never the sort of person that would have endeared himself to evangelicals but the world was a poorer place for his passing.

There was a science teacher in the school where I taught who used to tell his sixth form students the story of the Noble Prize winning physicist Neils Bohr's escape from Nazi-occupied Denmark to Sweden and then to England during the Second World War. I sometimes taught the same students and on one occasion I asked them if they had ever heard this particular story about Neils Bohr. There was widespread laughter. They had obviously heard it many times. One of the students remarked that the story grew with each telling. Clearly my science colleague was a master story-teller.

Men like my uncle and my science teacher colleague would have played a big part in preserving Jewish history. But it is also certain that Jewish story-tellers would have borrowed stories from the people around them, and transformed these stories so that the hero of the story would become an Israelite. We know there are stories in the Old Testament that have close parallels with the stories found among other nations. Noah and the Flood in chapters 6-8 of Genesis has a counterpart in the Babylonian *Epic of Gilgamesh*. The story of Joseph has an Egyptian counterpart in *The Tale of Two Brothers*. Imported stories, given a Jewish setting, would soon become part of Jewish folklore so that demarcation lines between purely Jewish stories and imported ones would be obliterated.

Story-tellers would tell the stories of the creation, Noah and the flood, the tower of Babel, Abraham, Lot and the destruction of Sodom, Isaac, Jacob, Moses, Joshua, Samson, Samuel, Saul, David, Jonathan, Elijah, Elisha and all the others, with all the stories, irrespective of their origin, being placed in a Jewish setting. And like all great story-tellers, they would embellish their stories. The best story-tellers of course would be the best embellishers.

Later writers would edit these well-known stories and arrange them into some kind of coherent structure to suit their own taste. To suggest that the final written version would represent inerrant fact and an actual history of anything is a massive leap of unjustified faith. What it did become is a part and parcel of Jewish culture, something that they all identified with, and this in turn would become the official version of their own history, and from this their own distinctive religion would, gradually, have taken shape.

A look at the stories of the ancient Israelites shows the mythical element that they contain. I will mention just two but there are many. The first story starts in Genesis chapter 18 and is a prelude to the destruction of Sodom and Gomorrah. In this chapter, Abraham receives three visitors. One is identified as the Lord and the other two as angels. When they take their leave, the Lord tells Abraham that "*The outcry against Sodom and Gomorrah is so great and their sin so grievous that I will go down and see if what they have done is as bad as the outcry that has reached me*" (v 20).

So, we are asked to believe that the Lord is not sure what is going on in the world that he has created and needs to go and investigate? Fine, if you know that what you are writing is just a story. Very odd, if you think you are writing absolute fact. This wonderful tale (and the subsequent destruction of the cities of Sodom and Gomorrah) is one that that would have given any half-decent story-teller a huge amount of scope for embellishment. The final written account that exists in our Bibles today is discussed a little later, from the standpoint of the inference that homosexuality was the sin that caused the destruction of these two cities.

The second story is found in Joshua 10:12-13. It tells of Joshua ordering the Sun and the Moon to stand still during a battle with the Amorites so that he could finish off the enemy before dark. No doubt the day had seemed a very long one, and no doubt a story-teller would not imagine that stopping the Sun was such a big deal, given that the Sun does not appear to be such an impossibly large object when viewed from the Earth. The writer would not be encumbered by any of the present-day knowledge that we have about the Sun and its size. And this embellishment would add some nice extra detail, and also attach a greater glory to the victory and surround the hero, Joshua, with a greater aura. Which victorious army has never embellished the account of a victory on the battlefield?

It is a story, however, that could never be told today. Now we know that for the Sun to appear to stand still it would need the Earth to stop rotating on its axis and then restart again sometime later. That does seem like an unrealistic proposition. If the Earth stopped rotating, a huge tsunami would be generated in the waters of the Mediterranean Sea (and every other sea). Poor Joshua and his army could well have been washed away as the waters swept all over the land of Israel. It might, on the other hand, have been very good for generating an enormous flood to sweep away all the sinners of Noah's generation.

Anybody in the fundamentalist churches (and many evangelical churches) who dares to query the factual accuracy of any of these accounts, however, would be regarded with astonishment and derision. You only have to listen to some of the preaching on the God Channel to know that many preachers lament the fact that there are some (other) preachers who do not accept that every word in God's Bible is absolute truth.

16   HOMOSEXUALITY IN THE
OLD TESTAMENT

Now I will turn to the critical issue of the destruction of Sodom in Genesis 19. The writer makes it abundantly clear that the real sin of Sodom is that of homosexuality or at least the practice of same-sex rape. The curious thing is that not one of the prophets of Israel seems to have heard of this particular slant on the story. None of the prophets, indeed, ever refer to the issue of homosexuality, even though some of them do mention Sodom and Gomorrah and they all rage endlessly against the sins of the people.

The most revealing reference by far is to be found in the prophet Ezekiel 16:49-50 where he says: "*Now this was the sin of your sister Sodom: She and her daughters were arrogant, overfed and unconcerned; they did not help the poor and needy. They were haughty and did detestable things before me.*" How strange that Ezekiel makes no specific mention of the sin of homosexuality here. Could it be that Ezekiel was not aware of the Genesis passage that we have today, that no such passage existed in his time? Was Ezekiel relying solely on oral traditions or a previous written tradition that did not survive or was supplanted by a newer, later version, and that these earlier sources made no mention of homosexuality? If that is the case, then this passage about homosexuality in today's Bibles must have come later, after Ezekiel's death, and would merely reflect the writers own homophobic views and those of the time in which he was writing.

Even Jesus has something to say about Sodom in Luke 10:12, but not in connection with homosexuality. He says that it will be more bearable on the day of judgement for Sodom than for the town that refuses to offer hospitality to his disciples who are being sent out to preach the Gospel. In the days before hotels and easily available accommodation, travellers often had to rely on the hospitality of ordinary people on the routes they travelled. Failure to show such hospitality to strangers was obviously regarded not only as an unacceptable breach of social etiquette but also a very serious sin. Perhaps it was even greater than the sin of homosexuality?

It should be mentioned that this story in Genesis emphasises the appalling attitude to women that existed at the time of writing. In Genesis 19:7-8 Lot says to the men of Sodom: "*Don't do this wicked thing. Look, I have two daughters who have never slept with a man. Let me bring them out to you and you can do what you like with them. But don't do anything to these men, for they have come under the protection of my roof.*" Clearly he did not think that he had much obligation to protect the welfare of his daughters. They were merely women and hence dispensable.

In Ian Wilson's 1985 book, *The Exodus Enigma*, he points out that some Old Testament stories appear to contain inauthentic detail, such as the use of coinage before the time when coinage apparently existed (it is only known to have existed from the time of the Lydians in the 7th century BCE) and also the use of camels before the time that they were first domesticated, around 1000 BCE. The belief of many evangelicals, and all fundamentalists, that things were written down as they happened does not really withstand close scrutiny. Indeed, the art of writing itself that is likely to have allowed literature as detailed as the Old Testament to be written at all is probably of much later origin than the historical setting of these stories. The Phoenicians developed the first widespread phonetic script which only became common around the 9th century BCE. It took a further two hundred years before the Greeks added vowels and the Iliad and the Odyssey were written. It is certain that the nomadic Israelites of the Exodus would not have kept detailed written accounts of their experiences in the desert over 40 years. They would have been too busy trying to survive.

It is pertinent here to refer to the only other occasions that homosexuality is mentioned in the Old Testament. There are two and they both occur in the book of Leviticus. Both are crystal clear and condemn any practice of male homosexuality out of hand. Leviticus 18:22 states: "*Do not lie with a man as one lies with a woman; that is detestable.*" Leviticus 20:13 states that "*If a man lies with a man as one lies with a woman, both of them have done what is detestable. They must be put to death; their blood will be on their own heads.*" The word "detestable" is rendered as "a perversion" in the RSV and "an abomination" in the King James Version. The lengths to which some well-meaning, gay-affirming Christians go in an attempt to try and find different nuances of meaning that would provide a "let-out clause" for the genuinely homosexual community shows a desperation to hang on to religious belief in impossible circumstances.

Paul's views on homosexuality were almost certainly formed by these very passages in the Old Testament. The Bible is a homophobic book and it would seem to me to be more honest to admit this fact and acknowledge that its views on this matter are no longer acceptable. This, of course, means admitting that it is not the Word of God and explains why the crusade against homosexuality, by many sections of the Church, is so unrelenting.

One fact of significant importance is that nowhere in the Old Testament do we find any reference to female homosexuality or lesbianism. There are two possible explanations of this. The first is that the male writers of the time of writing were not aware of the existence of lesbianism. In male dominated and polygamous societies, female homosexuality would either find no room for expression or could easily go undetected. The second possibility is that they did know but did not consider it to be of importance, since lesbianism in women would not been seen in the context of denying the purpose of sex, that is, procreation.

All of nascent life was thought to be contained in the sperm of the male. That was still the case among certain African village people when I was in Uganda in the late sixties and early seventies, and in many societies even today children are considered the possession of the father, not the mother, although this attitude has changed in the UK. It is odd, however, that the Holy Spirit should have been ignorant of female homosexuality or ignorant of the part that a woman played in conception. We have to wait until the New Testament and St. Paul before the issue of lesbianism is even acknowledged, and when it is, it is condemned in the same manner that male homosexuality is condemned.

It is also of interest to note that the God of the Israelites did not seem to approve of any sort of sex. In Leviticus 15:18 we find that there are problems if a man lies with a woman and has an emission of semen. Both become unclean, that is, rendered unfit to enter the presence of God. Perhaps the apparent distaste for sexual activity finds expression in the requirement of celibacy for Roman Catholic Priests.

The complete list of the seven Bible passages that specifically refer to homosexuality is given here, in the order in which they occur. Every one of these passages is condemnatory. The only one of these passages that specifically mentions what is now called lesbianism is in Romans 1:26.

In the Old Testament:
Genesis chapter 19; Leviticus 18:22 and 20:13.
In the New Testament:
Romans 1:26-27; 1 Corinthians 6:9-10;
1Timothy 1:9-10; Jude 1:7.

17   THE OLD TESTAMENT AND

JEWISH HISTORY

The Old Testament writers of Jewish history are not historians in the sense that we use this word today. Their object was not to record a factual account of events. It was rather to reveal God's dealing with his people through events in history. This of course leads to hopeless distortions. Reference to just two of Judah's kings will suffice to make the point.

The first king, Hezekiah, is mentioned in no less than three separate books of the Bible: 2 Kings chapters 18-20; 2 Chronicles chapters 29-33 and Isaiah chapters 36-39. The passages in Kings and Isaiah are, however, identical, indicating that one was copied from the other or that both used a common source. The second King, Manasseh, was Hezekiah's son. Both kings lived at the time when Assyria was the dominant world power, indeed could be claimed to have established the first great world empire. It was a time when their armies crushed all opposition with unbridled ferocity and barbaric cruelty. Sensible people saw little option but to accept Assyrian dominance and pay tribute. Reckless people took their chances, refused payment and almost without exception paid a terrible price.

Sargon II of Assyria died in 705 BCE and was succeeded by his son, Sennacherib, an event which precipitated rebellions in various parts of the empire. Each new monarch would have been faced with the problem of re-establishing the authority of Assyria as well as his own authority. Hezekiah was amongst the rebellious kings, forming an alliance with Egypt. His base was Jerusalem and he enlarged and strengthened the walls that fortified the city and built the famous Hezekiah tunnel for bringing fresh water into the heart of the city, a phenomenal piece of civil engineering for its time and one that would be a difficult enough challenge today. This amazing structure, preserved probably as it was on the day of its completion, now attracts hundreds of thousands of tourists every year.

According to the inscription contained on the famous Hexagonal Prism of Sennacherib, discovered in 1830 and now housed in the Oriental Institute in Chicago, Illinois, he also hired Arab mercenaries to help with the city's defence. Thus Hezekiah reversed the policies of his father, King Ahaz, who not only paid tribute to Tiglath-Pileser, the Assyrian monarch at the time, but also solicited his help to fight against Judah's enemies (2 Kings 16:7).

When, in 701 BCE, Sennacherib decided to teach Hezekiah a lesson and his armies swept through Judea capturing forty six cities and taking over two hundred thousand prisoners, as well as huge amounts of booty, help from Egypt did not materialise. One of the cities to fall was the city of Lachish, the second largest city in Judah and also a well-fortified one, although not as well-protected as Jerusalem. Nevertheless, this was sufficient to force the Assyrians into a major battle for its capture. There are Assyrian records of this campaign also to be found on Sennacherib's prism.

We know from Assyrian reliefs what befell hapless losers. They were butchered, impaled on stakes, roasted alive over fires, blinded and otherwise maimed.

Able-bodied people who were spared were carried off into slavery. Lachish was left with a remnant of a population, perhaps people deemed to be unfit for purpose. Even the Bible admits that Hezekiah panicked and sent a grovelling apology to Sennacherib at Lachish, together with as much booty as he could lay his hands on, including temple treasures (2 Kings 18:13-16). Sennacherib accepted the booty but still marched his army to the well-protected city of Jerusalem. There then follows an incident, the explanation for which is not known for certain. Sennacherib withdrew his army without taking the city, but claims that he left Hezekiah shut up in his city "*like a caged bird.*"

Perhaps the summer was ending and he wished to recuperate in the comforts of his capital, Nineveh, during the winter months, although there is the suggestion that an uprising had arisen there. The Bible's authors would have us believe that Sennacherib was assassinated by one of his son's as soon as he had returned home, greatly exaggerating the supposed deliverance. The truth is that Sennacherib does appear to have been assassinated by one of his son's, but not until 681 BCE, twenty years later. He spent much of his reign on great building projects and on beautifying his capital city.

The Bible authors make much of this "*victory of faith*" of Hezekiah, who had apparently been encouraged by the prophet Isaiah to stand firm because God would not let Jerusalem fall (2 Kings 19:6-7). What, however, of the fate of Judea as a whole, of the two hundred thousand or so other Jews who were not fortunate enough to be living in Jerusalem? Was their fate of no account? Did God's concerns extend no further than his own chosen city where his temple was situated? That, according to the Bible accounts, seems to be very much the case.

Hezekiah, who reigned for 29 years, made many religious reforms during his time, possibly because Judean prophets had blamed the northern kingdom's demise on its failure to be true to the God of Israel, and he is on the list of "approved" kings, kings who showed devotion to Yahweh (Israel's God). Indeed, 2 Kings 18:5 says of him: "*Hezekiah trusted in the Lord, the God of Israel. There was no-one like him among all the kings of Judah, either before him or after him.*" All this, despite the fact that at the beginning of Isaiah chapter 30, the prophet issues a warning to all those who would seek the help of Egypt, as Hezekiah did.

In contrast, Hezekiah's son, Manasseh, definitely did not trust in the God of Israel and is not on the approved list of kings. Manasseh reigned for fifty-five years, the longest reign of any Judean king, although the early years of his reign may have been as co-regent with his father Hezekiah. There are no Bible records of any wars during this period. Manasseh took the practical step of bowing to Assyrian supremacy and agreeing to pay regular tribute to the Assyrians to keep them at bay. He followed the policy of his grandfather Ahaz, who is criticised for changes made at the Jerusalem Temple "*in deference to the King of Assyria*" (2 Kings 16:18).

The truth is that Ahaz and Manasseh were pragmatic leaders. In those days, one of the obvious ways of showing deference to another ruler was to adopt the gods of that ruler, as well as paying tribute. It was not a religious issue as much as an attempt to avoid trouble.

Manasseh would have been aware of the devastation and the horrors that the Assyrians had visited on the land of Judah as a result of his father Hezekiah's rebellion. He could not hope to defy the Assyrians in battle and it was a case of "*if you cannot beat them, join them.*" He no doubt adopted the Assyrian religion wholesale. But he kept the peace. How easy for some fanatical religious zealot to criticise him at some later date, no doubt from a place of comparative safety, after the Assyrian empire was probably no longer in existence. Writing, of course, is not an activity that normally takes place in the heat of a battle. It is generally done from the safety of some ivory tower.

Manasseh reigned at a time when he had to face the reality of an all-conquering Assyrian war machine. He almost certainly lived in fear and is said to have sacrificed his own son in the fire (2 Kings 21:6). He is also accused of shedding a lot of blood. He was, no doubt, a typical tyrant. But it appears to be his failure to uphold the traditional religion of the Israelites that really condemns him in the eyes of the writer and he is described as having committed detestable sins and doing more evil than the Amorites. Indeed, his sins are such that the Lord, the God of Israel, is said to have declared: "*I am going to bring such disaster on Jerusalem and Judah that the ears of everyone who hears of it will tingle*" (2 Kings 21:12). These disasters did not occur during Manasseh's lifetime. The only disaster matching this prophecy is the fall of Jerusalem to the Babylonian armies many years later. So God does not necessarily punish the guilty. Anybody within four generations of the perpetrators of the crime will do, it seems, according to the second commandment, found in Exodus 20:4 and Deuteronomy 5:8 ". . . *for I, the Lord your God, am a jealous God, punishing the children for the sin of the fathers to the third and fourth generation of those who hate me . . ."* Was this written with hindsight, after the Babylonians sacked Jerusalem?

The God depicted in these accounts is a God who had no regard for the welfare of women or children, a God who used the most savage instrument of punishment by abandoning his people to the mercies of the warlike, barbaric Assyrians. It is difficult for us, from the relative safety of modern Britain, to imagine the sheer terror that must have been induced by these invading armies. A God whose purposes were carried out by these armies is a God of religious zealots, utter fanatics, a God of a people with tunnel vision and with a perspective that the Islamic Taliban would have little trouble in recognising.

The Old Testament prophets are little better than the historians. They can hardly find a good word to say for the people of Israel or Judah. Their writings are, in the main, one long diatribe about the evils of their society, and most of them look back on some supposed golden era that cannot be shown to have ever existed, not even in the Bible accounts themselves. The nearest thing to the kind of society imagined by these prophets is the society that they believed existed in the desert during the Exodus. Here everybody would have been in a similar situation with very little wealth. The fact that even in the desert, the Israelites were faithless and went after other gods the moment that Moses' back was turned, is conveniently overlooked. There would have been a semblance of equality that could never survive settlement in the Promised Land.

Settled societies have the opportunity to generate their own wealth, and some people will always generate more wealth than others. No settled society has ever managed to maintain equality amongst its citizens. It was this lack of equality, and the fact that the poor were very poor and were exploited by the rich and successful, that aroused prophetic fury.

The other issue that troubled the prophets was that of Idols and idol worship. The Old Testament gives no indication that the Israelites had much notion of monotheism. They lived in a historical period when people worshipped many God's and they were clearly no exception. Their own special God, Yahweh, may have been the most prominent one, and was the God that the prophets strove to establish as the only one, but they do not seem to have had much success and the truth is that monotheism was not established until after the fall of Jerusalem in 587 BCE and it may have been after the return from exile, some fifty years after this.

In the meantime, the prophets had to content themselves with warnings of impending doom, announcing God's forthcoming punishment on his disobedient people, a people who disregarded the Covenant that they were supposed to have with him and with each other. This they seemed to delight in doing. In Isaiah chapter 10, the prophet has God refer to the Assyrians as "*the rod of my anger, the staff of my fury!*" (v 5 RSV) and says that they will be sent against Mount Zion and Jerusalem because Jerusalem was full of idols (v 10-11) and the nation was godless (v 6). The Assyrians themselves are evil and will suffer their own punishment, but only after they had accomplished all the Lord's work against Israel (v 12).

The prophet Micah, probably a contemporary of Isaiah, shared the same opinion, declaring "*Zion will be ploughed like a field, Jerusalem will become a heap of rubble, the temple hill a mound overgrown with thickets*" (Micah 3:12). However, as we have already seen, Isaiah seemed to have a change of mind and decided that Jerusalem would, in fact, be spared (Isaiah 37:6-7). It was, of course, spared from the Assyrian attack in Isaiah's time, but Micah's prophesy came true when the Babylonians reduced Jerusalem to rubble over one hundred and ten years later.

There is no doubt that the prophets had a valid point. But if God was to destroy all nations where inequality was evident or where parts of the population did not worship him properly, there would not be a single nation left upon the face of the Earth. The prophets looked for an impossible ideal, and imagined that it had once existed in some distant past. In Jeremiah 6:16 the Israelites are advised to "*Ask for the ancient paths, ask where the good way is and walk in it.*" The good old days were always to be preferred to the present. Isaiah is an exception, because he looks forward to some golden era, and some of his most vivid prophesies are taken to refer to Jesus. But none of the prophets seems to have any regard for the times in which they lived. Indeed, they fit the image of the idiot in the Gilbert and Sullivan opera *The Mikado* who is described in the following terms:

"Then the idiot who praises in enthusiastic tone
All centuries but this and every country but his own."

This is not to say that the prophets did not have moments when they did express the deep longings within them and present these in exalted tones. In Amos 5:24, the prophet writes:

"But let Justice roll down like waters
And righteousness like an ever flowing stream." (RSV)

Micah wrote:

"And what does the Lord require of you?
To act justly and to love mercy
And to walk humbly with your God." (Micah 6:6 RSV)

Amid much doom and gloom, Hosea, in chapter 11 verses 8 and 9 has a momentary glimpse of a different God who says:

"How can I give you up, O E'phraim!
How can I hand you over, O Israel!
How can I treat you like Admah!
How can I make you like Zeboi'im?
My heart recoils within me,
my compassion grows warm and tender.
I will not execute my fierce anger,
I will not again destroy E'phraim;
for I am God and not man,
the Holy One in your midst,
and I will not come to destroy." (RSV)

These are beautiful thoughts, but seemingly wistful thinking rather than any word from God. Hosea prophesied shorty before the northern kingdom was crushed by Sargon II (722 or 721 BCE) and its people disappeared forever, victims of the Assyrian policy of intermingling conquered peoples in exile in order to obliterate national identity. Thus the greater part Abraham's descendants, who should all have been inheritors of the promises to Abraham, effectively vanished without trace. Just over one hundred and thirty years later the southern kingdom of Judah fell before the Babylonian onslaught (587 or 586 BCE).

Judah recovered because, unlike her unfortunate northern cousins, the inhabitants (at least enough of them) appear to have been allowed to live together as a group in or around Babylon, affording them the opportunity to preserve their separate identity. They were also allowed to go back to their homeland by Cyrus the Great, the Persian king who overthrew the Babylonians. Their temple based religion with its ritual and sacrifices was restored, and survived, with a few hiccups, until the Romans finally destroyed the temple and scattered most of the population in 70 CE.

Although most of this book has dealt with the problems regarding Christian belief, the issue is actually one of fundamentalist belief per se, the belief that God has revealed some eternal, unalterable truth to a member, or some members of the human race. I therefore include the present chapter to show that neither the Bible nor the Qur'ân can lay serious claim to being a revelation of any God to any member, or members, of the human race.

There are certain passages in the Qur'ân that Christians would find shocking. They would probably be more shocked to find similar (or even worse) passages in their own Scriptures. The first two passages are printed side by side to allow for a direct comparison. Others passages are dealt with separately as there is no direct comparison that makes as much sense.

Both of the passages in the table on the following page treat women as the property of men. In the Old Testament passage, women (even totally innocent ones) were made to drink some obnoxious potion of unknown strength and unspecified amount. The belief seems to have been that if she was innocent, the potion would not harm her. How many innocent Jewish women lost their lives for no more reason than that her husband was tired of her and had decided to "suspect" her of unfaithfulness? How many of them bribed the priests to make sure the wife did not survive?

The Bible	The Qur'ân
Excerpts taken from Numbers 5:14-28 (to keep it brief) . . . *and if feelings of jealousy come over her husband and he* **suspects** *his wife and she is impure—or if he is jealous and* **suspects** *her even though she is* **not impure**—*then he is to take his wife to the priest . . . Then the priest shall put the woman under oath . . .* [He is to say to the woman that *if* she has defiled herself, then] *May this water that brings a curse enter your body so that your abdomen swells and your thigh wastes away . . . He shall make the woman drink the bitter water that brings a curse . . . [emphasis added]*	**Sûrah 4 verse 34** *Men are in charge of women, because Allah hath made the one of them to excel the other, and because they spend their property (for the support of women). So good women are the obedient, guarding in secret that which Allah hath guarded. As for those from whom ye* **fear** *rebellion, admonish them and banish them to beds apart and scourge them. Then, if they obey you, seek not a way against them. Lo! Allah is ever High Exalted, Great. [emphasis added].*

The passage from the Qur'ân, displays an equally uncivilised attitude of an equally primitive age. An unreasonable man only had to **fear** rebellion from his wife to justify treating her in a barbaric manner. Men have never needed religious sanction to be violent towards women, as the battered wives in our own society clearly show. One can imagine the plight of women in any society where religious sanction for brutality does exist, as it does in many Islamic states under sharia law based on passages such as the one opposite.

The Afghan author, Khaled Hosseini, in his novel *A Thousand Splendid Suns,* draws attention to the misery that can be inflicted on women in such societies. How would any God at any stage of human development have ever trusted men with such power? The fact that there are (apparently) some more civilised passages in the Hadith (the unofficial sayings of Muhammad) regarding the welfare of women does not negate the fact some women will inevitably be brutalised with divine approval as a result of the existence of the passage quoted. The Qur'ân has no equivalent of the New Testament to ameliorate some of its harsh teachings, unless the Hadith is regarded as an equivalent.

The passages at the top of the next page both show another aspect of religious belief: the tendency to promote the message by inculcating extreme fear into the minds of the hearers The message is: this is what awaits you if you don't believe what I tell you and you don't do what I say. It relies on the fear of what might happen in the future to persuade people to adopt a particular lifestyle in the

Mark 9:47-48	Sûrah 4:56
And if your eye causes you to sin, pluck it out. It is better for you to enter the kingdom of God with one eye than to have two eyes and be thrown into hell, where	*Lo! Those who disbelieve Our revelations, We shall expose them to the Fire. As often as their skins are consumed We shall exchange them for fresh skins that they may taste the torment. Lo! Allah is ever Mighty, Wise.*
"their worm doth not die and the fire is not quenched" (Isaiah 66:24).	

present. It is insidious because no proof ever needs to be offered for the truth of this assertion: the merest possibility of it being true often provides sufficient persuasion of its own accord. Also, the particular lifestyle demanded is never a lifestyle agreed upon by those who have to participate in it. Rather, it is a lifestyle imposed by someone who claims to have received a message from on high with a divine right to impose the received notions on the world at large. No proof of the authenticity of these revelations can ever be provided, but unfortunately, neither can they be disproved. Once such beliefs take root, it takes inordinate courage to resist them. I have certainly heard many Christian preachers use exactly this technique when striving to convince unbelievers of the enormous danger in which they stand, unless they accept God's forgiveness forthwith.

My own feeling is that both these passages are the products of typically religious minds from distant, bygone eras. How can any sin be grievous enough to merit eternal punishment of this nature? What, exactly, does it say about any God who would sanction a punishment that, far from fitting the crime, exceeds it by unimaginable amounts? The truth is that it says nothing about any God but a great deal about ourselves, or at least about some over-religious zealots of long ago but whose spiritual descendants still live in our midst. It is no comfort to know that Jesus reinforces this view of God with his parable of the rich man and Lazarus (Luke 16:19-31).

I love my children. At times, however, they have disappointed me or they have made me angry and I have wanted to punish them. Occasionally I did so, although I cannot always claim that it was a godly or even a just punishment. Sometimes it was the result of my losing my temper and lashing out—occasions that I deeply regret. Fortunately (I think) I was more given to shouting than to physical violence, but I know that I said things in the heat of the moment that I regretted bitterly later on. Also, on one occasion that my children never let me forget, I repeatedly jumped on an apple in order to relieve my feelings.

However, I cannot remember it crossing my mind that I wanted them to suffer for ever on account of anything that they might have done. When my children suffer, I suffer too. I long for things to be made right between us. I am a father. Jesus referred to God as our Father. The idea of God as a father and a God who would countenance unending punishment do not sit easily together in my mind. I am now ashamed that

I have, in the past, listened uncritically to preachers who have sought to defend this "justice" of God. I wish to put it on record that I do not consider either of these passages to be the product of any revelation and the books that contain such passages cannot be, to my mind, divinely inspired.

The following passages, which are taken from the Bible, are mentioned to offer further evidence of the extreme intolerance, to say nothing of the primitive concepts, that we might expect from religious people of fundamentalist persuasion. Sadly, I have heard all of them used as texts for sermons supposedly illustrating some great truth about God and his just ways.

Numbers 15:32-36 and Numbers 25.

The first passage tells the story of a man who was found guilty of collecting wood for his family on the Sabbath day. On the orders of 'the Lord' he was taken outside the camp and stoned to death. We are not told what became of his wife and children who no doubt depended on him to fend for them. The second passage is rather confusing but also involves the killing of many Israelites who had fraternised with Moabite women and worshipped the "Baal of Peor".

Numbers 25:6-8.

This passage extols the virtues of a religious zealot named Phineas who saw fit to follow an Israelite into his tent and put his spear through both him and the Midianite woman with him. It was an action that caused the Lord's anger to turn away from Israel because it showed that Phineas was zealous for the honour of the Lord.

Numbers 31:1-18.

When the Israelites, towards the end of their long (forty years) journey through the desert, encroached on the land of Moab, they met with problems. Israelite men fraternized with Moabite and Midianite women who seduced them into worshipping the Baal of Peor. In chapter 31 we read that "the Lord" commanded Moses to take vengeance on the Midianites. Moses sends an army of twelve thousand Israelites into battle, but at the successful conclusion of hostilities, the army returns with women, young boys and young girls as captives. Moses is incensed that the intended total slaughter has not been carried out and that any of the Midianites have been allowed to survive. He orders all the women and boys to be killed, sparing only the girls who were virgins. Who was to verify the virginity of the girls?

Thomas Paine, in the 1795 volume of his book, *The Age of Reason*, refers to this sort of passage when he wrote:

"Whence arose the horrid assassinations of whole nations of men, women, and infants, with which the Bible is filled; and the bloody persecutions, and tortures unto death and religious wars, that since that time have laid Europe in blood and ashes; whence arose they, but from this impious thing called revealed religion, and this monstrous belief that God has spoken to man?"

I have read many apologetic defences of these passages in Numbers, none of which I have ever found remotely convincing. The simple truth is that they reveal barbaric views from a barbaric period of human history, and to invoke the name of God in all this must surely warrant the charge of blasphemy. I myself can only concur with the views of Thomas Paine.

The great tragedy is that these passages are at the heart of fundamentalist Jewish (Zionist) belief today. Some Jews (possibly many), are taught from an early age that the Palestinians are their enemies and they are taught to hate them. They are also taught that it is God's will that Israel's enemies should be destroyed. If Moses sanctioned such a thing, who is to oppose it? The Bible's lasting legacy is available for all to see in the terrible tragedy that is the Middle East and particularly the city of Jerusalem.

In passing, it is difficult to argue with an observation made by the French mathematician and Catholic philosopher, Blaise Pascal (1623-1662), that: "*Men never do evil so completely and cheerfully as when they do it from religious conviction.*" Indeed, nothing seems to stir up men to mindless violence and hatred as easily as religion does (although football has tried hard to be a rival in recent years). Witness the murder of homosexual people by Christian fanatics that occur in the USA. Witness the numbers killed or hopelessly maimed by American bombing raids in Iraq, after President Bush is reported to have claimed "*God told me to end the tyranny in Iraq.*" Witness the carnage caused by the destruction of the twin towers or the bombing of the London underground.

All of these atrocities were done with the support of religion and all of it indiscriminate, women and young children not exempt from the consequences. Some of it was done because of a promise of immediate reward in paradise. None of it, seemingly, was committed by those who actually promise this reward. They allow more gullible fools to be the immediate inheritors of these untold riches. The sentiments of this last Bible passage in Numbers, incidentally, find echoes in a verse of the Qur'ân, Surâh 8:67: *"It is not for any prophet to have captives until he hath made slaughter in the land."*

2 Samuel 24 and I Chronicles 21.

Both these passages recount the story of David taking a census of the fighting men of the Israelites. Samuel, however, says that God's anger burned against Israel and he (God) incited David to take the census. Chronicles says that it was Satan who was responsible for inciting David. Whichever way, God is incensed by this act, probably because it suggests a trust in human might, a trust in numbers, and hence implies a lack of faith. The authors may also have realized that knowledge of the size of the population allows the ruler to impose a system of taxation on that population and hence they may have preferred that such knowledge was not available in any period. What better way to dissuade a ruler from gathering this knowledge than to invoke the wrath of God on such an activity?

David is offered three options as a result of his sin: three years of famine, three months of fleeing from his enemies or three days of plague. David replies, *"Let us fall into the hands of the Lord, for his mercy is great; but do not let us fall into the hands of men."*

The result of trusting in God's mercy is that a plague is sent upon the people of Israel, delivered by an angel, and seventy-thousand of them died, although the people of Jerusalem seem to have been spared. The seeds of the idea of the special place of Jerusalem in the purposes of God are thus already evident in this passage. Plagues, of course, tend to kill the weakest members of society and children are particularly vulnerable. Neither are the women spared. David himself was aware of this and complains to God that he (David) is the one responsible, not the multitudes who have been slain.

The truth is that, in the absence of clean water supplies, no sewerage systems and, no doubt, poor hygiene among many of the population, plagues would have inevitably happened from time to time. Indeed archaeology appears to confirm that they did so, mass graves near ancient settlements having been found with no corresponding evidence of war damage. But, as we have already seen in the case of Paul and homosexuality, everything was viewed in relation to the will of God and the people's relationship to God, and any plague would have to be explained on the basis of this idea. When scientific knowledge was non-existent, what other explanation could be put forward?

Suffice it to say that this view of God does little for his image. No less a person than Jesus himself questions it on one occasion. In Luke 13:1-5, Jesus disputes the notion that certain Galileans, whose blood Pilate had mingled with that of the animals that they had sacrificed in the temple, or the eighteen people killed when the Tower of Siloam (in the southern part of Jerusalem) had collapsed on them, were more guilty that anyone else, or that they, by implication, were the victims of the wrath of God.

I have selected these passages because they very obviously raise questions over the whole idea of the inspiration of the Bible. They strongly suggest a viewpoint reflective of the age in which they were written. We cannot blame people for their ignorance. We can, however, be thankful for the knowledge that we have in our own day, and to lay aside this knowledge in favour of the ignorance of past ages, on the supposed basis that they had some revelation of God that has been denied to us, would seem to be the height of stupidity. This applies just as much to New Testament writings as it does to Old Testament writings.

The following passages are taken from the Qur'ân. I include them because it is important to realise that what I have written about the Bible, in my view, applies equally to the Qur'ân. This is because both the Bible and the Qur'ân are the products of supposed "revelations", things beyond rational discussion. You either believe it or you don't. The Qur'ân does not really contain passages in the same sense that the Bible does. There is no storyline, just an enormous collection of verses, most of which are to exhort the faithful and warn the unbelievers. The highest level of believer is the one willing to spend of their wealth and their lives in the service of Allah.

Surâh 4:95 (the context for this verse is one of military participation).

Those of the believers who sit still, other than those who have a (disabling) hurt, are not on an equality with those who strive in the way of Allah with their wealth and lives. Allah hath conferred on those who strive with their wealth and lives a rank above the sedentary. Unto each Allah hath promised good, but he hath bestowed on those who strive a great reward above the sedentary.

Surâh 9:83.

If Allah bring thee back (from a campaign) unto a party of them and they ask of thee leave to go out (to fight) then say onto them: Ye shall never more go out with me nor fight against a foe. Ye were content with sitting still the first time. So sit still, with the useless.

There are many references to fighting in the Qur'ân, and I found it impossible to read without acquiring the impression that Islam is a religion that fully subscribes to the idea of propagation of the faith by force and conquest. Christianity, of course, resorted to similar methods during the Crusades, Pope Urban II giving his encouragement and blessing to unholy conquest and slaughter, and rival Christian groups have continued on this path, on an intermittent basis, ever since the Reformation. It is, however, impossible to justify such actions from the New Testament. The Qur'ân is far closer in thought to the Old Testament.

I will end with one passage in the Qur'ân that indicates to me just how much the Qur'ân is the product of the human male mind rather than any revelation from heaven. It refers to the privileges for the prophet Muhammad and is found in the following passage:

Surâh 33:50.

"O prophet! Lo! We have made lawful onto thee thy wives unto whom thou hast paid their dowries, and those whom thy right hand possesseth of those whom Allah hath given thee as spoils of war, and the daughters of thine uncle on the father's side and the daughters of thine aunts on the father's side, and the daughters of thine uncles on the mother's side who

emigrated with thee, and a believing woman if she give herself unto the prophet and the prophet desires to ask her in marriage—a privilege for thee only, not for the (rest of) believers—We are Aware of that which We enjoined upon them concerning their wives and those whom their right hands possess—that thou mayst be free from blame, for Allah is Forgiving, Merciful."

The lifestyle of Muhammad appears to have been in stark contrast to that of Jesus who had "*nowhere to lay his head*" (Luke 9:58).

20   CONCLUDING THOUGHTS

In a sense, I have completed the journey that I set out on nearly a lifetime ago, a journey to discover the truth about life and about God. I began by accepting someone else's version of the truth and spent most of my life trying to gain a better understanding of that truth. However, when I was confronted with the stark reality of the fact that one of our children was homosexual, I was placed in a position where I needed clear evidence of the truth of what I believed

A God who detests homosexuality must be willing to "heal" homosexual persons. I needed my son to be "healed". Unfortunately, not only did God not seem interested in my son, he did not seem to have been interested in hundreds of others, boys and girls, men and women, who had desperately sought "healing" for themselves when they experienced same-sex attraction.

It was at this point that I was driven to adopt a more rational or "scientific" approach. Instead of assuming a particular truth at the start, I tried to see what truth the Bible might convey if I removed the pre-supposition that it was necessarily the Word of God. Unfortunately, this approach led me to one inescapable conclusion: there was no reason to imagine that there was any divine inspiration behind the Bible's message. I think that this conclusion became inevitable, in fact, as soon as I accepted that Paul had put forward a reason for homosexuality that was clearly false, given that homosexual children are as likely to be found in evangelical Christian families as among any other section of the population.

I suppose that I should have been left with a feeling of satisfaction that I had managed to arrive at a definite conclusion rather than being left in a world of uncertainty, waiting for the next world before I could discover any answers. Instead, I was left with a feeling of numbness, of emptiness, even of desolation. Seeking after truth clearly has a risk attached to it. There is no guarantee that the truth you find will be the truth you were hoping to discover, and in my case it certainly was not.

Whether the price of finding truth is worth the effort, therefore, is a matter of opinion. Maybe it is better not to know so that we can live in hope. That is precisely what my wife has chosen to do. She cannot detach her emotions from her intellect. The turmoil that our son's revelation caused left a raw area in her life and she cannot bear to revisit it. Bad news is best buried and forgotten. She has come to accept our son for what he is and she loves him as much now as she ever did. She avoids people who she fears will be judgemental and wants nothing more to do with any church. She has retained those parts of her faith that she is comfortable with. Whether or not there is any truth in what she believes no longer seems to be the point. It is what she wants to believe, and what she feels able to cope with.

I suspect that my wife belongs to the majority group among the human race. Drew Westen, a leading American academic, in his book *The Political Brain: The role of Emotion in Deciding the Fate of the Nation,* concludes from a study of numerous presidential (and other) elections that candidates whose campaigns concentrate of the "issues" tend to be far less successful than candidates whose appeal is to the emotions or to people's prejudices. Most people, it seems, vote from gut instinct, from loyalties often inherited from family, from feelings, or simply vote for those candidates who have slogans with which they can most easily identify. Far fewer appear to vote from any intellectual conviction.

Indeed, as most people would admit, the issues are far too numerous and complex for the majority to have any hope of acquiring an overall grasp of them. And what goes for politics also goes for religion, which is just as complex an issue and also an emotional one rather than an intellectual one. Nobody, confronted with the challenge to "make a decision for Jesus" is ever in a position to weigh up all the pros and cons. They consider a few of the central issues from the perspective of their own self-interest. How can anybody possibly know if what they are being offered is "the truth?" What is usually offered, incidentally, is in the form of "*believe what you can and accept the rest by faith.*"

We might hope that the people at the top, those responsible for making religion available to the many, would have some concern for truth. But they too have inherited their beliefs from others and rarely does anyone on the inside dare to question them. That is left to academic theologians whose opinions seem to be confined to their own circle, rarely reaching down to the masses. It is easier to go with the flow and accept what has always been accepted, as if longevity of belief confers legitimacy on that belief.

Who wishes to question the validity of two thousand years of custom and culture (and much more than that if you are Jewish)? The very identity of individuals and nations is often tied up with their religious beliefs and they are seen by many as an essential aid to stability and, indeed, civilisation. Truth has a low priority in the midst of such august considerations. As we have seen often enough, those who do dare to query established religious beliefs in the interests of truth, or for any other reason, do so at their own risk.

Is there any possibility of being able to answer Pilate's famous question, "*What is truth*?" In regard to religion, the answer is no. We could never be certain that we had arrived at the truth even if we ever did. We simply do not have any yardstick for deciding such matters. For the Christian, the written documents available present us only with a sea of uncertainty, upon which we are expected to make decisions that will affect us for all eternity. These uncertainties are not removed because particular groups of men arrogate to themselves the power to decide what truth people should believe, or worse still, seek to establish acceptable truth as they go along. Even if every living person accepted such "truth" it would not make any difference. The number of people believing something has no bearing on the validity of the beliefs.

Belief of the sort that is demanded of Christians should not have to rest on a story that is riddled with so many holes. Christianity, along with all other religions, is an expression of our desperate longing to find meaning and purpose in life, and of our willingness to believe in anyone or in anything that might possibly offer these things, even when our beliefs then have to be based on minimal and unreliable evidence. The Resurrection became a reality to the disciples because they desperately wanted to believe that their leader was still alive and still able to inspire them and empower them just as he had done when he was physically with them.

For all that, the power of belief cannot be denied, however misplaced some of it might be. Some misplaced beliefs are clearly better than other misplaced beliefs in that their overall effect results in a greater good, or possibly less harm, than might have been the case with some alternative. We would not want to return to times in which gods needed appeasing with human sacrifice. We can value the influence that religion has had on the lives of thousands who have lived sacrificially for the benefit of others, enabled by the knowledge that they themselves were loved by the God who created the world and that no circumstances could ever change that fact. Paul expressed this most clearly in one of his more famous passages: "*For I am convinced that neither death nor life, neither angels nor demons, neither the present nor the future, nor any powers, neither height nor depth, nor anything else in all creation, will be able to separate us from the love of God that is in Christ Jesus our Lord*" (Romans 8:38). If you have this belief, you may be able to move many mountains and you may be more than a conqueror in life. None of this, however, has any bearing on the truth of what is believed.

It is not only those we think of as great saints who can experience the value of belief. Thousands of ordinary people, criminals, prostitutes, drunkards, wife-beaters, frauds and every kind of ne'er-do-well have had their lives transformed by the power of the Gospel, the effect of belief. At the heart of the

Christian Gospel there is an immensely powerful message: there is a God who loves you, whose Son died for your forgiveness and whose Spirit will make his abode with you to help you through life's journey. This idea has inspired music of soaring beauty, poetry and great works of art and architecture. It has provided an immense source of comfort and strength to those struggling with grief, tragedy or inexplicable suffering. But, and this 'but' needs spelling out in huge letters: ***no amount of religious belief can change a person's sexuality, or restore sight to the blind, or hearing to the deaf, or mobility to the crippled, except, perhaps, in the most unusual and fortuitous of circumstances***. Even in areas where religion seems to play a significant role, we cannot always be sure that God is the only explanation for these experiences.

Furthermore, we cannot overlook the other side of the coin, where religion has been the instigator of the most murderous hatred and the most appalling deeds. Nor can we easily dismiss the dreadful and usually senseless suffering of people in earlier generations (or other places in the world today) when various plagues and all kinds of illnesses and afflictions attacked believers, unbelievers, men, women and children in an apparently indiscriminate manner. Many of these people looked to the God of Jesus for deliverance but found that he did not answer, despite the promises of Jesus regarding prayer referred to earlier. Death was not necessarily quick but often involved a protracted period of intense suffering, exacerbated by the fact that nobody ever knew what caused the problem and nobody had any idea how to relieve any of the symptoms, let alone effect a cure. Today, we are spared much of this, not because of faith but because of knowledge.

While confronting the claim made by evangelicals for an inspired Bible in some form or other, I have also had to confront my own experiences of forty years as a believing evangelical/charismatic Christian. How much of my own experience was I sure of? The truthful answer to that question is very little, or probably none. That is because everything was dependent on belief. You can never question these beliefs, because the moment you do you will be cut off from the God who sustains you. Thus, I was encouraged to believe that I had been saved, because the word of God promised it. If you believe it for long enough, and others believe it with you, you eventually come to accept it. It becomes part and parcel of your life.

Likewise with the experience of the "Baptism with the Holy Spirit". Babble away and believe that you have been baptised in the Spirit. "Babbling" is not quite as bizarre as it may seem, for when the mind is concentrated on God, it can be a wonderful form of emotional release. This "feel good" factor can easily be identified with a special blessing from God, and seems particularly convincing when accompanied by an induced state of emotional frenzy. But one has to ask if this is anything very different from the induced frenzy experienced by the North American Indian tribes who danced around the totem pole to prepare for battle or to induce rain to fall. The only difference is that you *believe* that you have been touched by the power of God and this, supposedly, validates the experience. You believe and keep believing, because you know that the moment you cease to believe, you lose everything. God himself will disown the unbeliever. You believe that, as a committed follower of Jesus, you are guided by the Holy Spirit, proof of which fact is never necessary. However, as observed in my first book, when the Church really could be said to be in need of being "led by the Spirit" (a favourite phrase of the Bishops), the Spirit does seem to be very conspicuous by his (her?) absence.

What of the beliefs that I held? My vision of Jesus was one of my own formulation. He was a person that I never met and I had scanty information about; little more, in fact, than a snapshot of his life. My image was built up from an acceptance of the things that I liked and a neglect of the "hard sayings" that I was not so keen on or did not understand. My image of Jesus was an image that I could be comfortable with.

I liked the idea of a miraculous Jesus who was both loving and all-powerful, who could be counted on as a trusted friend, who could empower me to be an "overcomer" and could be relied upon to pick me up when I fell. I liked the Jesus who opposed the religious hypocrisy and bigotry of his time and demanded a change from within, a change of the heart. I liked the idea of a kingdom where love prevailed and strife and jealousy would be absent. I liked the Jesus who wept over Jerusalem, a Jesus who did not rejoice in what he saw as the inevitable consequences of Jewish intransigence, in contrast to many evangelical Christians who seem to rejoice at the thought of the ultimate punishment of the heathen. I liked the Jesus who would take charge of my life, because then I need not worry about the future. I liked the idea of having a guaranteed a place in heaven.

But the Jesus who seemed to demand a fanatical devotion even to the disregard of family? Possibly, before I got married and had children, but not so appealing afterwards. It was also something I could not ask him about. I could only make up my own mind and trust that I was being "led by the Spirit".

The snapshot of Jesus that we have is, in the end, incomplete and sometimes seems contradictory. It was provided by people from a very different age to that in which we now live and in no sense can it be trusted as a historically reliable picture or indeed as a reliable interpretation of the significance of his life. I find it hard to believe that a God who bothered to visit the planet or send his son to do so, would then leave behind so many question marks, so much uncertainly, and yet demand unswerving faith in, say, a resurrection that is so haphazardly presented in the recorded accounts of the Gospel writers and St. Paul. I could never be sure whether the image that I had of Jesus was the same as anybody else's image. The same has to be said for all Christians.

In the end, we all form our own version of whatever religion we adopt (if we adopt any), or we adopt somebody else's beliefs because we are too lazy to form our own. Of course, for thousands of years, almost everybody was dependent on being told exactly what to believe. People who could not read would have no access to any knowledge. When John (the Apostle?) writes in 1 John 2:27 "*As for you, the anointing you received from him remains in you, and you do not need anyone to teach you*" he seems to overlook the fact that the Holy Spirit cannot work with nothing. He can only work with the knowledge we possess. And most people down the ages would have had to acquire that knowledge from someone else, as they would have had no means of teaching themselves. Today, nearly all of us are dependent on the translation work of others for any of our knowledge. The accuracy of the translations is something over which I have no control—I am obliged to trust the translators and I am indebted to them.

Writing this book has been a valuable exercise for me because it has caused me to think carefully about what I really do believe and to examine the ground upon which I have constructed these beliefs. It has enabled me to clarify many issues that had previously been muddled together in some incomprehensible manner. This is important, particularly where my beliefs may have consequences for others, such as the LGBT community.

As my wife and I have continued to make friends among this group of people, we have found them to be as decent and friendly as the Christian community. Many may have personal issues, issues resulting from feelings of rejection and of being marginalised by society, feelings of worthlessness, sometimes feelings of self-loathing, feelings of being an abomination to God for being the way that they are. That, however, has as much to do with attitudes in society and particularly among Christians as it has with anything else. The good news that I would like to bring to all these people is that there is no firm evidence of a God who finds them an abomination. Indeed, there is no firm evidence of any God at all, no evidence that there is any divine authority who sanctions an absolute code of moral values. Moral values are simply reflections of the rules that any group of people, living together in a community, agree to adhere to for the perceived benefit of the whole group. They have no significance beyond that, no eternal permanence.

Neither my wife nor I find the LGBT community an abomination. In fact, the people that I now find to be an abomination are the homophobic religious bigots in positions of leadership who choose to trumpet their uninformed views under the guise of serving the interests of some God of their own making. They do not proclaim the great Christian virtues of faith, hope and love (1 Corinthians 13:13). Instead, they offer ignorance, bigotry and condemnation. Many politicians, in their search for votes, are every bit as ignorant and guilty as their religious counterparts, and are more than happy to sacrifice truth for expediency, no matter who gets hurt in the process.

It is sometimes said that to gain anything worthwhile, at some stage it is necessary to take risks, to launch out in faith. I took the risk and have lost my faith. Perhaps this is preferable to living with beliefs that are dubious and which separate me from others who do not share those beliefs. I have not tried to argue whether religion is a good or a bad thing. My question has been, rather, how much credibility can be given to the idea of revealed religion and in particular to the idea that the Bible is the product of such revelations? I do not even claim to answer the question "Is there a God?" But if there is, I can say only that neither I nor anybody else can make any credible claim to know him.

The Bible is, nevertheless, a great book because at its heart is a timeless story, a story that deals with something central to human aspirations: our longing for freedom. We crave freedom from war and fear;

freedom from oppression and slavery; freedom from hunger and want; freedom from illness and disability; freedom to govern ourselves, freedom of belief, freedom to discover truth for ourselves and to determine our own destiny. Some of its passages have a great beauty, even in translation. But the Word of God? Sadly, I have had to abandon the beliefs I held for forty years. To believe that the Bible really is the Word of God, or to believe that that the claims of any "revealed religion" have validity is to require a leap of faith that I now realise is totally unwarranted. This, at least, should be good news, if not for me then at least for my son and indeed for all homosexuals everywhere. To him and to them, I offer my unreserved apologies.

If any evangelical was to read this account, they would be horrified that anyone, after a lifetime of belief, could contemplate tossing aside his salvation as if it was of so little consequence. This implies, however, that belief retained "just to be on the safe side" has some value. Real belief of the sort that might lead to "salvation" is something quite different and pervades every area of life and thought. This kind of belief is impossible to sustain if ever you become convinced that your beliefs have no proper foundation and your God suddenly disappears, or fails to show up with any answers, in a time of crisis.

One thing struck me on this journey, and that is that one lifetime is insufficient for any mortal to come to a rational choice between competing religious claims, or even become properly acquainted with all of them, unless the decision is that since a rational choice is impossible then all religions are equally likely to be false. For the whole of one's future in eternity to depend on having made the "correct" choice in whatever lifetime one is granted, now seems to be an utterly preposterous idea. It is one more reason why I can no longer subscribe to my original beliefs.

Despite this end result, I have no regrets about what I have done, except to say that there is an inevitable sense of loss. I wish that the Bible had conveyed a different message and had never mentioned homosexuality. Or I wish that everything was much more black and white and that homosexuality did not exist, that God really had made everybody "male or female" as Genesis 1:27 (a verse that Jesus quotes) implies. Sadly, that is not the world that exists. To have any integrity, I must live in the world that does exist, not in some fanciful world that I wish existed. The real world is one of endless complexity, one riddled with unfairness and injustice, and where nature sometimes makes tragic mistakes, with unfortunate consequences for some human beings. Not everybody is as "*fearfully and wonderfully made*" as the psalmist claims to have been (Psalm 139:14). We are a long way from a full understanding of the human condition.

I must now try to construct some new meaning to my life. At least I will have the consolation of knowing that I will not be constructing a meaning that will come at the expense of one particular group of people who, like me, just found themselves here, were not asked what kind of sexuality they would prefer, and must therefore make the best of the hand that life has dealt them. I wish all of them well, and in particular, I harbour the wish that the family dislocations that may have occurred as a result of preconceived and false notions surrounding the whole area of human sexuality finally become a thing of the past.

We have made slow progress in trying to overcome superstitions and prejudices of all kinds; to move to more enlightened views of issues ranging from witches, slavery, race, skin colour, equality of the sexes, left-handedness, disability of various kinds and now to sexual orientation. It is time to acknowledge that some people happen to be homosexual (or bisexual or transgendered) and for the rest of us (and particularly many sections of the Christian community) to get over that fact and learn to accept all people for what they are instead of trying to force them to conform to what we erroneously think they ought to be.

The author, David Robert-John, can be contacted at davidrobert-john@hotmail.co.uk. Every effort will be made to reply to genuine questions.

The author also intends to create a Webpage. This should be easily located by typing David Robert-John into any search engine (such as Google).